THE SUFFERING SERVANT

**TOUCHSTONE
TEXTS**

Stephen B. Chapman, Series Editor

THE SUFFERING SERVANT

Isaiah 53 for the Life of the Church

J. GORDON McCONVILLE

Baker Academic
a division of Baker Publishing Group
Grand Rapids, Michigan

© 2023 by J. Gordon McConville

Published by Baker Academic
a division of Baker Publishing Group
Grand Rapids, Michigan
www.bakeracademic.com

Printed in the United States of America

Library of Congress Cataloging-in-Publication Data
Names: McConville, J. G. (J. Gordon), author.
Title: The suffering servant : Isaiah 53 for the life of the church / J. Gordon McConville.
Description: Grand Rapids, Michigan : Baker Academic, a division of Baker Publishing Group, [2023] | Series: Touchstone texts | Includes bibliographical references and index.
Identifiers: LCCN 2023010927 | ISBN 9781540960634 (cloth) | ISBN 9781493442911 (ebook) | ISBN 9781493442928 (pdf)
Subjects: LCSH: Bible. Isaiah, LIII—Commentaries. | Servant of Jehovah.
Classification: LCC BS1515.53 .M394 2023 | DDC 224/.107—dc23/eng/20230616
LC record available at https://lccn.loc.gov/2023010927

23   24   25   26   27   28   29   7   6   5   4   3   2   1

To Gordon J. Wenham

Contents

Series Preface

In writing workshops, "touchstone texts" are high-quality writing samples chosen to illustrate teaching points about compositional techniques, genre conventions, and literary style. Touchstone texts are models that continually repay close analysis. The Christian church likewise possesses core scriptural texts to which it returns, again and again, for illumination and guidance.

In this series, leading biblical scholars explore a selection of biblical touchstone texts from both the Old Testament and the New Testament. Individual volumes feature theological *exposition*. To exposit a biblical text means to set forth the sense of the text in an insightful and compelling fashion while remaining sensitive to its interpretive challenges, potential misunderstandings, and practical difficulties. An expository approach interprets the biblical text as a word of God to the church and prioritizes its applicability for preaching, instruction, and the life of faith. It maintains a focus primarily on the biblical text in its received canonical form, rather than engaging in historical reconstruction as an end in itself (whether of the events behind the text or the text's literary formation). It listens to individual texts in concert with the rest of the biblical canon.

Each volume in this series seeks to articulate the plain sense of a well-known biblical text by what Aquinas called "attending to the way the words go" (*salva litterae circumstantia*). Careful exegesis is pursued either phrase by phrase or section by section (depending on the biblical text's length and genre). Authors discuss exegetical, theological, and pastoral concerns in combination rather than as discrete moves or units. They offer constructive interpretations that aim to transcend denominational boundaries. They consider the use of these biblical texts in current church practice (including the lectionary) as well as church history. The goal of the series is to model expositional interpretation and thereby equip Christian pastors and teachers to employ biblical texts knowledgeably and effectively within an ecclesial setting.

Texts were chosen for inclusion partly in consultation with the authors of the series. An effort was made to select texts that are representative of various biblical genres and address different facets of the Christian life (e.g., faith, blessing, morality, worship, prayer, mission, hope). These touchstone texts are all widely used in homiletics and catechesis. They are deserving of fresh expositions that enable them to speak anew to the contemporary church and its leaders.

Stephen B. Chapman
Series Editor

Acknowledgments

I suppose the book of Isaiah has been with me, one way or another, all my life. At first, this was just by virtue of its firm place in the Christian spirituality and worship in which I was brought up. It provided language and ideas then in ways that I was scarcely aware of. In time, I found it to be one of the Bible's wonders: monumental, mysterious, delightful, sobering, and profoundly challenging. It has been a privilege to teach it over many years and, in recent times, to have had the opportunity to write both a commentary on the whole book and now this volume on Isaiah 53 in Touchstone Texts. Together, they represent my best shot at saying what this great book can mean for the Christian church. For both these opportunities, I am extremely grateful to Jim Kinney and his excellent colleagues at Baker Academic. And for the present series, I am much indebted to Stephen Chapman for inviting me to contribute to it and also for his careful, perceptive, and learned editing.

Like everyone for whom the Bible has been a lifelong companion, I have not read it alone, but with a great company of witnesses too many to name or even remember (*o tempora!*). In these latter days, they include members of St. Matthew's

Church, Cheltenham, who meet as a home group: Malcolm and Sybil Catto, Trevor and Margaret Cooling, Bill Harvey, Charlotte Jamieson, Anne Jones, Andrew Meakin, Ceri Settatree, Rachel Wadsworth, my dear wife, Helen, and, in memoriam, Gwen Harvey, Harold Jones, and Ralph Settatree. They also include members of the group we simply call the Symposium: Dee Carter, David Evans, Andrew Lincoln, John Richardson, and Robert Walker; and former colleagues, like me retired, but who still rejoice in chewing the theological cud: Fred Hughes, Nigel Scotland, and Gordon Wenham (and Andrew Lincoln again). I am immensely grateful to all of these for sharing with me in the unending task of listening to Scripture as we try to walk the Christian way together.

I pick out two of the above for special mention. My wife, Helen, has not only had a quiet but profound influence on all my thinking for the last fifty years, but also for the past six or more has had to share me with Isaiah—a ménage that was especially intimate during the years of COVID lockdown! She has been unfailingly supportive and is entitled now to look forward to Isaiah's retirement.

Gordon Wenham was my doctoral supervisor, my first and most important guide in the arts of biblical research, later a colleague at the University of Gloucestershire, and for many years has remained a firm friend. He is a model of both deep scholarship and humble service, and as he approaches (I believe!) his eightieth birthday, I dedicate this volume to him in fond gratitude.

A Note on Presentation

The exposition of a biblical text is inevitably indebted to a massive history of scholarship and translation. I set out in chapter 1 some of the implications of this for the interpretation that follows. The translation of the text of Isaiah 53 in chapter 3 is my own. Any fresh translation of a biblical book in English enjoys the luxury of knowing that many others are also available to the reader for comparison. Apart from chapter 3, I have in general defaulted to NRSV.

Biblical chapter and verse references are according to standard English versions. Where the Hebrew numbering varies from the English, this is indicated in the format Isa. 9:2–7 [9:1–6].

Abbreviations

Old Testament

Gen.	Genesis	Eccles.	Ecclesiastes
Exod.	Exodus	Song	Song of Songs
Lev.	Leviticus	Isa.	Isaiah
Num.	Numbers	Jer.	Jeremiah
Deut.	Deuteronomy	Lam.	Lamentations
Josh.	Joshua	Ezek.	Ezekiel
Judg.	Judges	Dan.	Daniel
Ruth	Ruth	Hosea	Hosea
1 Sam.	1 Samuel	Joel	Joel
2 Sam.	2 Samuel	Amos	Amos
1 Kings	1 Kings	Obad.	Obadiah
2 Kings	2 Kings	Jon.	Jonah
1 Chron.	1 Chronicles	Mic.	Micah
2 Chron.	2 Chronicles	Nah.	Nahum
Ezra	Ezra	Hab.	Habakkuk
Neh.	Nehemiah	Zeph.	Zephaniah
Esther	Esther	Hag.	Haggai
Job	Job	Zech.	Zechariah
Ps(s).	Psalm(s)	Mal.	Malachi
Prov.	Proverbs		

New Testament

Matt.	Matthew	Acts	Acts
Mark	Mark	Rom.	Romans
Luke	Luke	1 Cor.	1 Corinthians
John	John	2 Cor.	2 Corinthians

Gal.	Galatians	Heb.	Hebrews
Eph.	Ephesians	James	James
Phil.	Philippians	1 Pet.	1 Peter
Col.	Colossians	2 Pet.	2 Peter
1 Thess.	1 Thessalonians	1 John	1 John
2 Thess.	2 Thessalonians	2 John	2 John
1 Tim.	1 Timothy	3 John	3 John
2 Tim.	2 Timothy	Jude	Jude
Titus	Titus	Rev.	Revelation
Philem.	Philemon		

General

BCOT	Baker Commentary on the Old Testament	esp.	especially
ca.	*circa*, about, approximately	i.e.	*id est*, that is
cf.	*confer*, compare	no.	number
chap(s).	chapter(s)	Syr.	Syriac
e.g.	*exempli gratia*, for example	Tg.	Targum
		v(v).	verse(s)

Bible Versions

BHS	*Biblia Hebraica Stuttgartensia*	NIV	New International Version
CEB	Common English Bible	NJPS	*Tanakh: The Holy Scriptures: The New JPS Translation according to the Traditional Hebrew Text*
ESV	English Standard Version		
JPS	Jewish Publication Society Tanakh		
KJV	King James Version	NRSV	New Revised Standard Version
LXX	Septuagint		
MT	Masoretic Text	RSV	Revised Standard Version
NASB	New American Standard Bible	Vg.	Latin Vulgate

Qumran / Dead Sea Scrolls

| 1QIsaᵃ | Great Isaiah Scroll |

Rabbinic Works and Tractates

| b. | Babylonian Talmud |
| Ber. | Berakhot |

1

Introduction

The text before us is properly designated as Isaiah 52:13–53:12. I will explain why this is so in due course. Mostly, we will refer to it as Isaiah 53, which is a convenient and recognizable shorthand. So when you see "Isaiah 53," please take it to mean Isaiah 52:13–53:12.

Isaiah 53 contains a stunning portrayal of a man who has suffered beyond measure. He was so scarred by his torments that other people could barely look at him, and they turned away. We are given no clue as to what had reduced him to this state, but his wretched appearance made his isolation even worse. Surely, people thought, someone so extraordinarily marred must have been singled out by God for terrible punishment. This image of a human person in great affliction is rivaled in the Old Testament perhaps only by Job, whose friends thought he too was being punished by God. There are also expressions of extreme distress in certain psalms, in which sufferers speak in their own voices; Psalm 88 is a prime example, with its terrible closing cry of abandonment to lonely darkness. But Isaiah 53 gives us a view from outside, as it were. On the part of the speakers who saw him in his anguish, it is retrospective, for they have come to realize that they had catastrophically misunderstood him (53:4). Far from indicating God's displeasure, his suffering actually had a profound purpose in God's mind: nothing less than the salvation of those who had spurned him.

What changed their minds? The story unfolded in Isaiah 53 does not stop with the image of dereliction in verses 2–3; rather, it has a remarkable outcome. The unfortunate victim is "like a lamb that is led to the slaughter" (53:7 RSV), and he has evidently suffered to the point of death (vv. 8–9). Whether he actually died is implied rather than explicitly stated, a point to which we will return in due course. But he does, unexpectedly, have an afterlife: "He shall see his offspring, he shall prolong his days" (v. 10 RSV). And there is more to this than mere survival—or even resurrection. For those who once thought him a reprobate have also begun to penetrate into the meaning of his life. This unlikely man has been made "an offering for guilt," a kind of sacrifice; he will "make many righteous" and even "bear their iniquities" (53:10–11). The whole picture, indeed, is framed with assertions of his exaltation and reward: "He shall be exalted and lifted up, and shall be very high" (52:13 RSV); and "[the LORD] will divide him a portion with the great" (53:12 RSV).

This, then, is the man introduced to the reader only as the LORD's "servant" (52:13). Resemblances to the story of Jesus will be obvious to any who know the Gospels, and it is no surprise that the earliest Christians, who knew this text as part of their Scripture, should have taken it to point to him. It has even been doubly canonized in Christian thought and worship, not least through George Frideric Handel's great oratorio *Messiah*. Perhaps more than any other single part of Scripture, Isaiah 53 has taught Christians who Jesus was and how he became the savior of the world. In the present volume, we aim to consider how the great poem helps unfold this central theme of Christian belief.

To that end, however, we hope to read it, not simply as a stepping stone on the way to the revelation of Christ, but also for its enormous power of expression and its sheer impact on the reader.

Isaiah 53 and Jesus

When the risen Jesus walked with two disciples to the village of Emmaus, "he interpreted to them the things about himself in all the scriptures" (Luke 24:27 NRSV). They did not recognize him as they had talked along the way, but only when he broke bread with them in a house in the village. Then they reflected on how deeply moved they had been as he had expounded Scripture to them. Their glad recognition of the risen Christ was bound up with their realization that their Scriptures, which they certainly knew well, had come to a wonderful fulfillment in him.

Is it possible that Isaiah 53 was one of the texts Jesus used in explaining to them the real significance of who he was? A number of New Testament pointers show how important it became to the early Christians in helping them understand who Jesus was and what he had done. Prominent among them is the apostle Philip's encounter with the Ethiopian royal official returning home after worshiping in Jerusalem, whom Philip finds puzzling over Isaiah 53 (Acts 8:26–40). What had brought this highly placed Ethiopian to worship in Jerusalem, and how he came to be reading Isaiah, are intriguing questions that the text leaves unanswered, apart from the clear indication that the Spirit of God was somehow in these events. So here is this foreigner reading about a person he knows nothing about:

> Like a sheep he was led to the slaughter,
>   and like a lamb silent before its shearer,
>   so he does not open his mouth. (Acts 8:32–33 NRSV;
>   Isa. 53:7)

Just as we do not hear the words of Jesus on the Emmaus road, we do not hear how Philip explained the text. But Philip was living in the searching light of the recent resurrection and ascension of Jesus, and we read that "he told [the official] the good news of Jesus" (*euēngelisato autō ton Iēsoun*; Acts 8:35). For him, this text was "gospel," or "good news" (*euangelion*), about the "sheep led to the slaughter," which spoke powerfully to him about these overwhelming events and told him that they had always been in the mind of God.[1]

So the episode casts a bright light on how the Spirit of God worked in deepening the disciples' understanding of their vocation to bring the gospel of Christ to the whole world. It is the Spirit who prompts Philip to go to the man in the chariot and ask him, not what he is reading, but if he understands it. And when the man has been baptized and has gone on his way rejoicing, the Spirit takes Philip further on his missionary journey. At the heart of this transformational moment is the interpretation of Scripture and its focus on the man Jesus.

Luke (the author of Acts) also tells in his Gospel of the wise old Israelite Simeon. It is Simeon who, when Mary and Joseph bring the child Jesus to the temple for his dedication, takes him in his arms and declares his joy at having witnessed for himself, in this child, the fulfillment of God's ancient promise of salvation to Israel. His sense of completion is such that he utters the prayer that has become known to the church as the Nunc Dimittis, a supreme expression of a life fulfilled and a readiness for death (Luke 2:29–32). Most importantly, the prayer shows how Simeon's deep knowledge of Scripture, hand in hand with

1. There is a scholarly question about the ways in which New Testament texts refer or allude to Isa. 53 and how they interpret it. For example, does Luke's citation of Isa. 53:7 imply that he meant the whole context to be understood by the reader, including Christ's atoning death for sin? Questions of this sort will be addressed in chap. 4 below.

revelation by the Holy Spirit (2:26), is brought to bear on his intense experience of the work of God. The words of the prayer have strong resonances with Isaiah 40–55, and most notably 52:10, part of the immediate prelude to chapter 53.

What these three stories have in common (all, as it happens, from the writings of Luke) is their testimony to how the first Christians came to a new understanding of their familiar Scriptures, finding their deepest meaning in the life, death, and resurrection of Jesus. How did this happen? Crucially, they were rereading their Bible in the light of Jesus's resurrection and ascension. They had come to believe that their crucified and risen Lord was indeed the Christ. And this set them on the challenging path of reading the Scriptures from a Christian point of view. They did not yet call that Scripture the "Old Testament"; it was still simply their Bible, which had taught them everything they knew about God. But now their understanding, led by the Spirit of God, had irrevocably changed. This did not mean that it was suddenly fully formed, however. These disciples had merely set out on what would be a long journey of reflection and learning. The fulfillment of the Scriptures in Jesus would have the effect of driving them back to those Scriptures, to keep deepening and feeding their apprehension of him. Traces of their growing understanding of the "suffering servant" are heard in other parts of the New Testament, such as 1 Peter 2:23–24. And this path of deepening perception continues still.

So is the servant figure at the center of Isaiah 53 to be identified as Jesus? When these verses were first penned, they had no such reference. The book of Isaiah was written for audiences who lived several hundred years before Jesus, and for whom it was intended to make sense in their own world. To say, therefore, that Isaiah 53 speaks about Jesus raises unavoidable questions about how the Old Testament became Scripture for

Christians, and specifically how, along with the New Testament, it became a witness to Christ.

Like any other part of the Bible, Isaiah 53 did not simply appear from nowhere. It had a place in the history of ancient Israel and a literary context in the book of Isaiah. As a text, it was also subject to a history of reading and rereading, attested through the various forms in which it has come down to us. This textual history is evidence in turn of its susceptibility to ongoing reinterpretation at the hands of those who received and transmitted it. It is important to say something about each of these elements as we prepare to think about how the text comes to speak of Christ.

Isaiah 53 in Its Contexts

The History of Israel

The prophet Isaiah lived and preached in the eighth century BCE, a time when the northern kingdom of Israel succumbed (in 722 BCE) to the might of the great Neo-Assyrian Empire, never to reappear on the pages of history. The southern kingdom of Judah, however, with its capital in Jerusalem, survived into the time of Babylonian ascendancy in the regions of Mesopotamia and Palestine, in the sixth century BCE. In 587 BCE, Jerusalem and its temple were laid in ruins by the devouring armies of King Nebuchadnezzar. Many people from Judah were carried off into exile in Babylonia, while many others were left behind in a ravished land. In the minds of Judeans, this was the deepest cut of all, not just in material and economic terms, but in their sense of themselves as the favored people of their God the LORD. It is to this period of history that chapters 40–55 of Isaiah primarily relate. They address people, in both Judah and Babylon, who are wounded by their losses and in need of reassurance that their God would, and could, still be faithful to them. This concern echoes through the pages of Isaiah 40–55. This historical context is not just accidental or of secondary importance. It was in these circumstances that Isaiah 53 first meant something both to whoever composed it and to its first hearers and readers. This is so even though we do not know enough of the history to be sure about the precise historical setting of the poem, as we shall see in a moment. Theologically, the essential point is that God's self-revelation in Jesus Christ comes within history, and specifically the history of Israel. Why do things that happened in a small country in Iron Age Palestine matter for an understanding of Jesus and the Christian faith? There have been voices within Christianity over the years who have answered this question by saying: They do not matter at all! Yet these have been a minority report. The church broadly has held on to the Old Testament alongside the New as part of God's witness to Christ. Why this should be so is hidden in the mystery of divine providence. It is bound up with the Christian belief that God has become present to humanity within human history. Jesus was a Jew, and as such he stood within the flow of Jewish history. Apart from this, it is impossible to make sense of the New Testament, as we have already seen in regard to Simeon and Anna and their recognition of the baby Jesus as the promised Messiah.

This still invites the question of how to read Isaiah 53 in such a way as both to respect its ancient context and to interpret it in the light of Jesus. We will have this question before us as we proceed.

The Book of Isaiah

The literary context of the book of Isaiah is inseparable from the historical one. Isaiah contains prophecies that derive from both the Assyrian and the Babylonian period as well as that of the Persian Empire, which ousted and succeeded the Babylonian Empire in 539 BCE and continued on into the fourth century BCE. One of the key figures in Isaiah 40–48 is the Persian king Cyrus II, who is named in 44:28 and 45:1 and depicted as one whom the LORD raised up to restore the ruins and temple of Jerusalem, and the exiled people to their land. (The same view is expressed in Ezra 1:1–4.) The contents of the book therefore address events spread over several centuries. For most modern interpreters, this means that the book was written, not all at once, but by different authors who wrote in different periods. In modern scholarship on Isaiah, the three imperial periods are mapped onto three parts of the book: chapters 1–39; 40–55; and 56–66. That division is now recognized as oversimplified, as the book as a whole is a profound reflection on the work of the LORD in Israel over the course of those centuries, and its ultimate production was the result of a complex process that cannot be completely reconstructed. However, the focus of chapters 40–55 is indeed the imminent reversal of the LORD's own rejection of his people by means of Babylon, and their restoration through Cyrus.

The story of this dramatic change in Judah's fortunes is carried by many of the book's prophetic sayings. An important turning point, for example, is chapter 35. But most of the key sayings are in chapters 40–55, not least their famous opening:

> Comfort, O comfort my people,
>   says your God.
> Speak tenderly to Jerusalem,
>   and cry to her
> that she has served her term,
>   that her penalty is paid,
> that she has received from the LORD's hand
>   double for all her sins. (Isa. 40:1–2 NRSV)

These words declare that the LORD means to save his people. He will do so in spite of the long period of punishment that they have endured; he will repair the broken city and temple and restore the exiled people to their land (40:9–11; 44:26–28). He will do these things in the face of their great doubts about his will and power to accomplish them (40:27). It is to address this crisis of faith that the powerful rhetoric of Isaiah 40–55 has been composed.

Crucially for our understanding of Isaiah 53, a second figure, besides Cyrus, plays an essential part in this vision of a bright future for Judah. This is the one the LORD calls "my servant," first introduced in Isaiah 41:8. The same designation, as we have seen, is given to the suffering figure in Isaiah 53 (at 52:13). The Suffering Servant, therefore, belongs within the developing motif of the servant of the LORD in Isaiah 40–55. The servant's portrayal in these chapters is indispensable background to chapter 53.

Who, then, is the servant? The word "servant" is applied in the Old Testament to anyone whom the LORD calls to his service for any purpose, even, in one place, to King Nebuchadnezzar (Jer. 27:6)! In Isaiah it is used of the prophet himself (Isa. 20:3), the temple official Eliakim (22:20), and King David (37:35). In Isaiah 40–55, however, "servant" takes on a new and special function. In 41:8 and in several other places, it refers to "Israel," or "Jacob," as a whole (notice also 44:1–2; 45:4; 49:3). These historic names are applied to what is in effect the remnant of ancient Israel that consisted (when the prophecies were written) of the people of Judah, both those who had been exiled and those who remained in the land. In this way the (then) present and future communities are said to be the true heirs of all the ancient promises to Israel, and especially of the status of the LORD's chosen people.

How can the identification of the servant of the LORD as the whole body of Israel possibly be related to the vivid image of a suffering individual in chapter 53? This conundrum may be addressed in several ways. One classical critical solution was to isolate as separate compositions certain passages in chapters 40–55, including chapter 53, in which the servant was most readily understood to be an individual, and to designate them "the Servant Songs" (42:1–4; 49:1–6; 50:4–9; 52:13–53:12). This is now rightly thought to underestimate the organic development of the motif throughout chapters 40–55. At the other end of the scale, it is sometimes held that the corporate idea of servant-Israel should be maintained, even where the appearance of an individual is strongest. In this way, the man who suffers at the hands of others, and for the benefit of the "many," would be consistently a metaphor for the suffering and mission of Israel. More persuasive, in my view, is the attempt to hold together both aspects: there was a man who suffered in fulfillment of a specific vocation from God, and in doing so he took upon himself the larger, ancient mission of Israel to the world. Isaiah itself shows a resolve not to allow the two poles of the image to be separated. This is most evident in 49:3–6, where the servant is first identified with Israel (v. 3) but then is said to have a mission *to* Israel (v. 6).

As I noted above, the idea of the servant of the LORD undergoes an organic development within Isaiah 40–55. The servant begins as Israel, called many generations earlier in its forebear Abraham (41:9). The purpose of Abraham's calling, according to Genesis, was that from him a people should come who would have a home in a land that God would give them. In them, moreover, "all the families of the earth" would be blessed (Gen. 12:1–3). The mission of servant-Israel in Isaiah is expressed in slightly different terms, yet it evidently taps into the same theological memory. The Isaianic servant is to "establish justice in the earth" (Isa. 42:4), be a "light to the nations" (42:6; 49:6), and act as witness to the LORD's unique saving authority in the world (43:10). The portrayals of the servant that seem to refer to an individual are woven into this developing narrative. How this works out in chapter 53 is a matter to be explored in the more detailed analysis below.

At this stage a question remains: If indeed the servant is portrayed both as an individual and collectively as Israel, who is the individual in view? We have noticed that Isaiah 40–55 has a certain historical setting, and also that its poetry aims to show its hearers how they should think of God and themselves in relation to that setting. The Babylonian exile and the Persian king Cyrus were historical realities. Does it not follow that the servant must originally have been an individual who also lived then, and whose fate had some bearing on the lives of the exiles and the people of Judah? This is part of the question already raised about the way in which events in Israel's history prior to Jesus become relevant to how we understand Jesus himself.

As to who was originally meant by the servant, this is one of those questions to which we cannot give a convincing answer. A number of suggestions have been made. Could it have been Jeremiah, the "weeping prophet" whose life spanned the end of the kingdom of Judah and part of the exilic period? He was certainly oppressed and threatened by segments of his own people, and he used language about himself very similar to that in Isaiah 53:7 (Jer. 11:18–20, esp. v. 19; see also 20:10, 14–18). Could it have been King Jehoiachin, carried off as a captive to Babylon by King Nebuchadnezzar in 597 BCE and imprisoned until the "thirty-seventh year of his exile"? Jehoiachin's release at that time by the magnanimous act of a new king (2 Kings 24:10–17; 25:27–30) might have looked like a kind of afterlife following a long period of anguish.

Or, perhaps most plausibly, was it the prophet himself whose voice is heard in Isaiah 40–55? This might be suggested, for example, by a certain similarity between the call of Isaiah in Isaiah 6:1–8 and the scene in 40:6, in which an unidentified speaker responds to a voice calling him from heaven. It is widely supposed that Isaiah 40–55 stems from the ministry of an exilic prophet unknown to us by name and so commonly called Deutero-Isaiah. Isaiah 40:6 may then intend to show a connection and continuity between the eighth-century Isaiah of Jerusalem and this sixth-century prophet. Another intriguing association between the prophetic speaker and the servant is at Isaiah 48:16: "And now the LORD God has sent me and his spirit" (NRSV). This reminds us of 42:1, where God is said to have put his spirit on the servant. It also echoes 49:1–6, where the speaker, ostensibly the prophet, is addressed by God as "my servant" (49:3). And in 50:4–9, the same speaker (presumably) is violently persecuted for his role in passing on the teaching of God.

While each of these suggestions has merit, Isaiah 53 itself does not give us enough to confine its meaning to a single individual. This is hardly accidental. When we align it with particular people who have suffered and been vindicated, such as those just named, it will, not surprisingly, have certain resonances simply because it depicts a profound human experience. The poem, therefore, rests on a paradox: it has an undeniable historical setting and reference, yet its capacity to refer is not nailed down and exclusive. As a matter of poetic strategy, the figure of the Suffering Servant has apparently been left open to be applied wherever it seems appropriate to do so.

The Text of Isaiah 53

When we read Isaiah 53 we are reading a specific, given text. This might seem too obvious to say. However, anyone who has carefully compared different English Bible translations of any text will have noticed how they often vary, sometimes significantly. Some of these variations are due to the fact that the translators have followed different versions of the Hebrew or Greek text. Readers of the Old Testament in English may also have observed occasional notes in the margins of their translation, which point out that a particular phrase has been taken, not from the Hebrew, but from the Greek, and less often from other ancient languages. (I am looking at the RSV of Isa. 48:10–11 as I write this, which has "corrected" the Hebrew in v. 10 and adopted the Greek and Latin in v. 11.) While the Old Testament texts were composed in Hebrew,[2] they were translated for the benefit of certain ancient Jewish audiences into their languages.

One such audience was the large Jewish community that lived in the Hellenistic Egyptian city of Alexandria. They were part of the Diaspora that had spread far and wide in Africa and western Asia following the Babylonian exile. These Egyptian Jews spoke Greek, and most did not understand Hebrew. Naturally, they wanted to know what their Scriptures had to say about themselves and their destiny. Learned scribes among them therefore translated the Hebrew text into Greek, creating what we know as the Septuagint (or LXX). Since the scribes almost certainly had before them versions of the Hebrew text that we no longer possess, their translations are indirect witnesses to

---

2. That is, apart from the few chapters that were written in Aramaic: Dan. 2:4b–7:28; Ezra 4:8–6:18; 7:12–26. Jewish exiles in Babylon evidently adopted the dominant Aramaic language. The language problem that came with the spread of Jews around the world is illustrated in Neh. 8:6–8, where returned exiles need to have the Hebrew Scriptures translated for them.

those versions, besides the ones that we do possess. This means that, in principle, LXX might preserve better, or more "original," readings than the Hebrew text that was later adopted as standard. Such instances illustrate a key point about the biblical text: we do not possess a perfect or "original" text, but only a range of ancient versions of it, among which we are bound to select what we regard as the best. One of the essential tools of biblical scholarship is textual criticism, which has developed techniques for making such decisions. Modern translations all owe a debt to such scholarship.

As readers, therefore, having no access to a pristine "original" text, we are brought into a process of reading and interpretation that goes back to the time when the earliest texts we have were being produced. The translators of LXX often made decisions about theological meaning. In Isaiah 53 this is evident, for example, in LXX's frequent use of the Greek word *doxa*, "glory," in places where its Hebrew equivalent does not appear, evidently expressing a theological conviction that the servant figure evinced something of the glory of God. These translators also expressed the concept of sacrifice for sin differently than the Hebrew Bible. While the Hebrew in Isaiah 53:10 reads "When his life [soul] is made a guilt offering, he will see offspring and prolong his days," LXX has "If you [plural] give for sin, your soul shall see long-lived offspring." Likewise, in verse 11 of LXX, it is apparently the LORD, rather than the servant, who makes many righteous. Both of these differences seem to detract from the idea of the servant's atoning sacrifice.[3] These are important theological points, and we will return to them in the fuller analysis below. We should bear in mind that we do not know for sure what Hebrew text the LXX translators

3. So also Hengel and Bailey, "The Effective History of Isaiah 53 in the Pre-Christian Period," 125–26.

had in front of them. But we can see that the ancient text gave rise to major theological questions, which faith communities seem to have wrestled with in their attempts to understand the Scriptures.

While Jews in Alexandria were making sense of their Scriptures in the Hellenistic world, so too were Jews in Palestine. Palestinian Jews became rather diverse in the years between the return from exile and the coming of Jesus, a diversity in which biblical interpretation played a major part. One important group was the community that settled in the dry and relatively remote location of Qumran on the shores of the Dead Sea. These were sectarians who had distanced themselves from the religious authorities at the Jerusalem temple and saw themselves as the rigorous and authentic form of redeemed Israel. Their scribes made copies of biblical books and produced other writings, which, since they began to be discovered in 1947, have become known as the Dead Sea Scrolls.[4]

Among these is the oldest Hebrew text of Isaiah that we possess, the Great Isaiah Scroll, which is held by the Shrine of the Book in Jerusalem.[5] In Isaiah 52:14 this manuscript has a verbal form, spoken by the LORD, that appears to mean "I anointed" and is closely related to the word meaning "messiah." This is instead of a similar-looking word in the commonly accepted Hebrew text, which means something like "marred." The Qumran form makes poor sense in context and looks like the intrusion of a messianic reinterpretation of the servant figure. It is likely that the Qumran scribes understood the text to refer to a founding figure in their community known as the Teacher of Righteousness, and they no doubt saw themselves as his disciples.

4. For a general introduction, see VanderKam, *The Dead Sea Scrolls and the Bible*.
5. It is usually designated 1QIsa\u1d43.

This messianic interpretation also appears in the Jewish Targum (Tg.) of Isaiah, a slightly later paraphrastic translation of the biblical text into Aramaic, which refers to "my servant the messiah" in 52:13.[6]

I have referred just now to "the commonly accepted Hebrew text" of the Old Testament (or as some prefer, the Hebrew Bible). By this I mean the text known as the Leningrad Codex, so called because it is housed in a library in St. Petersburg (formerly Leningrad).[7] This text is dated to around 1000 CE. It may seem odd that the commonly accepted text is over one thousand years later than the Great Isaiah Scroll at Qumran. But this makes an important point: we use a text that has passed through many hands. The Leningrad Codex is an exemplar of the Masoretic Text (MT) tradition. The Masoretes were Jewish scholars who preserved the Hebrew Bible over many centuries, copying and recopying manuscripts. A comparison of the Leningrad Codex with the Qumran Isaiah scroll shows relatively few divergences between the two, which testifies to a remarkable uniformity in the transmission of the Hebrew Bible over a very long period after biblical times, without the benefit of the printing press. The MT, however, is also a witness to the fact that we as modern readers inherit a text that has always been subject to reinterpretation. The new thing that the Masoretes brought to their task was the invention of a system of vowels (and other signals to the reader) for a text that was originally consonantal only. They did this to establish authoritative conventions for reading Scripture aloud in the synagogue. But in doing so, they inevitably made interpretive

6. Tg. Isaiah is dated between 70 and 135 CE by Ådna, "The Servant of Isaiah 53 as Triumphant and Interceding Messiah," 189–90.

7. This codex provides the textual basis for the modern critical edition of the Hebrew Bible known as *Biblia Hebraica Stuttgartensia* (or *BHS*), published by the Deutsche Bibelgesellschaft.

and theological decisions about correct readings of potentially ambiguous words and phrases.

The quest for an original text of Isaiah 53, therefore, has something in common with the quest for the historical individual known as the servant. We have no access to the original text, yet it is necessary to work with a concept of such a text, embedded in historical reality. This idea lies behind the judgments we make about what might have been the original reading at any point. In reading we are, as it were, drawn into a conversation with a long line of readers whose beginnings lie hidden from us in the distant past. We would possess no text at all if this were not so. In what follows, we will see more of what generations of readers have made of it. This is an inevitable part of interpretation. But it does not follow that the meaning of the text is merely relative. This is why it is indispensable to hold to the concept of an original, or "best," text as a bulwark against fanciful or untenable interpretations.

Isaiah 53 in (and outside) the Biblical Canon

I have been arguing that Isaiah 53 is not a stand-alone text but has certain contexts that must be accounted for in its interpretation. The last of these contexts is the whole Bible, or, more accurately, all the Jewish and Christian literature up to and including the New Testament. This topic overlaps with that of the development of the text since, as we have seen, ancient versions of it (such as LXX) already testify to theological reflection within Jewish believing communities. But there is a further layer of this sort of development in Jewish writings that allude to and interpret Isaiah 53.

It is clear that the authors of biblical books written later than Isaiah knew Isaiah 53 and sometimes allude to it. The prophet Zechariah lived after the exiles had begun to return to

Jerusalem and was one of those who encouraged the rebuilding of the temple (Ezra 5:1–2). In Zechariah 12:10–12, he speaks of a lamentation among the people of Jerusalem over one "whom they have pierced" (Zech. 12:10). This is reminiscent of the penitence of those who came to realize their error in condoning the vilification of the servant in Isaiah 53. It looks as if Zechariah knows the Isaiah passage, and that the figure of the Suffering Servant has entered the people's corporate memory as a kind of "martyr messiah."[8]

In another late writing, Daniel 12:3, people known as "the wise" are said to "turn many to righteousness," recalling Isaiah 53:11: "By his knowledge he made many righteous." Here, the memory of the servant feeds a new understanding during a time of martyrdom that God will ultimately vindicate his faithful people in resurrection after death.[9]

The apocryphal Wisdom of Solomon, extant only in Greek and written probably in the first century BCE, uses the Isaiah text in its own way.[10] The book presupposes a situation of persecution that cannot be exactly identified, and the author wants to demonstrate the ultimate vindication of godly people, in contrast to the wicked. It thus takes up the Old Testament motif of perplexity at the suffering of the righteous and the better outcomes in life that often seem to come to the unscrupulous (cf. Ps. 73). Wisdom finds an answer in justice that comes after death. Two passages link this theme expressly to Isaiah 53. In Wisdom 2:12–20, some people who are characterized

---

8. Hengel and Bailey, "Effective History of Isaiah 53," 88.

9. The book of Daniel appears to have been written in the second century BCE and influenced by the terrible persecution of Jewish people in the time of the Hellenistic king Antiochus IV Epiphanes, who desecrated the Jerusalem temple in 167 BCE. In the resistance to Greek rule that followed, many Jews died.

10. The fact that it exists in Greek suggests an Alexandrian audience, like LXX. Yet it may have been known to Palestinian Jews as well. See Horbury, "The Wisdom of Solomon," 653.

generally as "the wicked" show their resentment against "the righteous" (*ton dikaion*), a generic reference to a righteous person. They mock the idea that he is a "servant of the Lord" (*paida kuriou*, 2:13). The word *pais* may be translated "child" or "servant," but the phrase's echo of the servant of the LORD in Isaiah 40–55 (41:8; 42:1; 53:11),[11] together with the theme of his violent persecution, indicates that the Suffering Servant of chapter 53 is in mind. This is reinforced by Wisdom 5:1–8. Here the wicked, facing a final judgment for their sins, stand amazed at the strange and unexpected nature of salvation (5:2), meaning the salvation of the righteous person they had despised and derided (5:4). They now see their grave mistake (vv. 6–8), like the people who speak as "we" in Isaiah 53:1–6. The text is plainly a reflection on Isaiah 53. It is applied, however, in a distinctive way. The people who come to see the reality of the fate of the righteous do not evince repentance, but rather look back in dismay only when it is too late. The Wisdom author has used Isaiah 53 to serve his theological purpose of showing a general vindication of the righteous after death.

Texts such as Zechariah 12, Daniel 12, and Wisdom 2 and 5 testify to habits of biblical interpretation that prevailed in the late Old Testament period and continued into the New. They reveal the intellectual climate in which, for example, the evangelist Luke did his interpretive work. And Luke was not the only New Testament writer who reflected on Isaiah 53. Mark knew that Jesus gave his life "as a ransom for many" (Mark 10:45), in an apparent allusion to Isaiah 53:11–12. Matthew found a fulfillment of Isaiah 53:4 in Jesus's healings (Matt. 8:17). John's Gospel takes up the idea of the servant's exaltation (Isa. 52:13) and, notably, LXX's emphasis on the word *doxa*, "glory," to make his link between Jesus's crucifixion and his glorification

---

11. The word *pais* is used for "servant" in these texts in LXX.

(John 12:28, 32). Paul alludes to Isaiah 53:4–6, 11–12 in Romans 4:25 to speak of Christ's atoning death and his resurrection. He also draws on Isaiah 52:15 as grounds for his preaching the gospel (Rom. 15:21). Paul is influenced again by Isaiah 53 in the great christological hymn in Philippians 2:6–11, in which Christ "emptied himself" and took the form of a servant, only to be finally exalted. I shall say more about these texts below (chap. 4). For now, I simply note that these writers, like the others I have mentioned, knew no difference between "what it meant" and "what it means." For them Isaiah 53 shed light on who Jesus was, and Jesus shed light on the meaning of the text.

▓ Conclusion

We embark on our consideration of the magnificent poem in Isaiah 52:13–53:12 with a paradox. On the one hand, the passage is embedded in an actual history, with a reference, presumably, to an individual whom its earliest readers would have recognized. It was a time in which much was at stake for a particular Jewish community that was coming out of long years of oppression and exile and that longed for a return to freedom and prosperity as a people in its own land, worshiping God at a restored temple in Jerusalem. These were the terms in which they thought of salvation or redemption. In this context, the servant played a key part.

On the other hand, we encounter the poem within a long history of theological interpretation. I have tried to trace this in an illustrative way. Christian reception of it is part of that history. This is not something to be apologetic about, but rather arises inevitably from standing within God's history, and particularly because of the Christian belief that the life, death, and resurrection of Jesus Christ are the key to understanding that history.

The New Testament's appropriations of the passage, and of the Old Testament generally, are not tendentiously superimposed on a more "authentic" version. Rather, they belong organically within the whole history of the formation and transmission of the writings that came to form first the Hebrew canon, then the Christian one. That is, the New Testament interpreters received authoritative texts in relation to the ever-changing environments that Christians inhabited, and to the events that perpetually challenged them to understand God, themselves, and the world in new ways. Christians today are their heirs in this respect. The obverse of this is that Christian readings exist alongside others, notably, Jewish ones, whose relation to the ancient text is in principle the same.

A further word must be said about Jewish readings in particular and the stance of the present study toward them. It should be clear from the account so far how deeply Isaiah 53 is rooted in Jewish history and thought. What Christians call "the Old Testament" is for Jewish readers their Scriptures, the Hebrew Bible. They are the natural inheritors of this body of Hebrew literature that has deeply affected their history and culture, and indeed language, to the present day. Christian readings of the Old Testament, therefore, must always be conducted in full cognizance that there is also the Hebrew Bible, that Christians do not exclusively "own" these wonderful texts. Early Christian interpreters felt a need to wrest the Scriptures from Jews, to try to prove to them that the canonical texts pointed unequivocally to Jesus as the Messiah. Justin Martyr's second-century *Dialogue with Trypho* is the classic example of this, in which the Christian apologist attempts to defeat his imaginary Jewish interlocutor by persuasive argument. In our day, and with due regard to the terrible history of the oppression of Jews in Christian countries, the pursuit of such a zero-sum game is plainly inappropriate.

Christian reading of Scripture must acknowledge the rights of Jewish reading, in an atmosphere of mutual respect. In practice, Old Testament/Hebrew Bible scholarship has become a shared enterprise, and at its best there can be fruitful interaction between Christian and Jewish perspectives.[12]

This idea of a unified Scripture (understood in different ways by Christians and Jews) rests on a belief that it has been given in the context of divine providence. The present volume is intended to read Isaiah 53 as one of the great texts of the Christian canon, and therefore it will try to unfold its significance in that context. For Christians, Isaiah 53 has been found to speak cogently about the life, death, and resurrection of Jesus. The transmission and interpretation of the Scriptures, viewed from one perspective, have been subject to the vagaries of history. Yet from another perspective, they are a gift from God, formed in such a way as to witness to the truth that is in Christ. One can view this under the banner of the canon, formed over centuries as faith communities perceived how the writings given to them taught them to think about God.[13] We might equally point to the concept of divine inspiration, following 2 Timothy 3:16. The relationship between canon and inspiration has a controversial history, but they can be understood to be in harmony with each other if the authority of Scripture is held to reside in the text itself, being the product of the Spirit of God working in and through all the human labors that made the Scriptures what they are.[14]

12. See Brettler and Levine, "Isaiah's Suffering Servant," who treat Isa. 53 with an eye on both Christian and Jewish perspectives. They call for close attention to the text and its context, then document postbiblical Jewish readings as well as New Testament ones.

13. This point is finely argued by Christopher R. Seitz, most recently in his *The Elder Testament*. Seitz takes a cue from Brevard S. Childs, especially his *Biblical Theology of the Old and New Testaments*.

14. Stephen Chapman offers a detailed argument for the recovery of the concept of inspiration that reckons fully with the history of the canon's formation. In contrast to the view that inspiration must occur in the mind of a specific human author, the

It is for theological reasons like these that it is essential to pay attention to the particularity of the Hebrew text of Isaiah 53 as it has been received. That text had an actual genesis in a specific historical, social, and political matrix about which we know a certain amount (as described above). Its broad historical setting is the turning point in Jewish history when the Babylonian exile was coming to an end. Its sociological setting is the kind of society found in the late Iron Age in Palestine, organized around a temple-city with ancient royal associations but subject to a succession of imperial powers. These settings carry with them a host of assumptions about human relationships, as we shall see in the fuller analysis below. The point bears upon both the nature of God's relationship to historical events and God's involvement with his covenant people Israel. Attention to the text in itself is an essential reference point for all other readings and a safeguard against fantastic interpretations.

It will, therefore, be our main task in what follows to consider Isaiah 53 very carefully. In doing so, we shall discover a kind of dialogue between the received text and the interpretations to which it has given rise, leading us, I hope, to appreciate something of its genius. For it is the particularity of its words and phrases, often because of their ambiguity and elusiveness, that generates theological reflection on the topics it raises. Such reflection is by no means uniform. On the contrary, from ancient to modern times there has been lively debate over important theological questions, including the following: Was the servant an individual or a community? Could his suffering on behalf of others be called "vicarious" or "substitutionary"? Such terms need careful definition.[15] Does the accent fall on

locus of inspiration is removed from author to text, while retaining the text's rooting in history ("Reclaiming Inspiration for the Bible"). The topic of inspiration has also been addressed by Levison, *Inspired*.

15. I will say more about this in chaps. 3 and 4.

his suffering or on his ultimate triumph? Was he a messianic figure? Did he actually die and rise from the dead? The New Testament itself bears witness to this ferment of interpretation. Some topics remained contested even after the biblical period. Not the least of these is what it means to say that Christ died for sinners (Rom. 5:8).

2

The Form of Isaiah 53

Isaiah 53 as a Unit

Isaiah 53 has become a key text for Christian interpretation by virtue of its importance in the New Testament, and for the ways in which it is understood there to refer to the life, death, and resurrection of Jesus Christ. Of course, no New Testament writer described the text before them as "Isaiah 53." Ancient readers of the Scriptures apparently felt no need to divide their familiar texts into chapters. When Jesus read from Isaiah in the synagogue in Nazareth, he did not look up "Isaiah 61:1–2," but rather "he unrolled the scroll and found the place where it was written" (Luke 4:17). Similarly, the quotation of Isaiah 53:7–8 in Acts 8:32–33 is introduced with "The passage of the scripture that [the eunuch] was reading was this." The chapter divisions that we are accustomed to were established only in the medieval period, and they are usually attributed to Stephen Langton, archbishop of Canterbury from 1207 to 1228. While they are a generally useful guide, they do not always match perfectly with the best subdivisions of the biblical text. As I have already indicated, when we say "Isaiah 53" we actually mean Isaiah 52:13–53:12. Our text, therefore, is a good illustration of the point.

What is it, then, that marks out Isaiah 53 as a definable text? While our familiar chapter divisions date from the thirteenth century, there were a number of older systems of organizing the biblical text.[1] Most importantly, the Masoretes, the scribes who produced the received Hebrew text of the Old Testament, had a method of paragraphing as part of their guidance for synagogue reading. The close of a paragraph was marked by the letter *p* or *s* standing after the end of the final line of the sense unit.[2] These letters are still printed in editions of the Hebrew Bible. Like our chapter divisions, they depend on judgments about what constitutes a sense unit, and readers may or may not always agree with them. However, it is significant that such a paragraph marker stands after Isaiah 52:12 in MT, and the next one is after 53:12. The Masoretes, therefore, regarded 52:13–53:12 as a sense unit.

There are good reasons to take a cue from the Masoretes on this point. A reader of the book of Isaiah quickly discovers that it is composed of many individual units, including short prophetic pronouncements (as in Isa. 5), narrative sections (chaps. 7–8, 36–39), and more connected stretches of speech, as in chapters 40–55. How these came to be put together in a single book has long been a topic of scholarly investigation. Within Isaiah 40–55, the discourse flows somewhat smoothly, so that breaks between sections of text are relatively weak. But there are certain features of this portion of the book that enable us to talk about discrete units.

In the case of Isaiah 53, the most obvious is the theme of the servant of the LORD. The dramatic development of Isaiah 40–55

---

1. For antecedents to Langton, see Saenger, "The Anglo-Hebraic Origins of the Modern Chapter Division of the Latin Bible."

2. The letters stand, respectively, for "open" and "closed." No appreciable difference between the two remains in practice.

is a little like those modern films in which the scene switches back and forth between different parts of the storyline. The camera leaves the heroine in danger in order to catch up on the progress of the police investigation. Then, the tension heightened, the focus returns to her, and we immediately pick up from where it broke off. Just before our text, in Isaiah 52:1–12, one of the other strong themes of this part of Isaiah is coming to a climax, namely, the LORD's salvation of Jerusalem (or Zion) and the end of the time of exile. The final verse of that section, 52:12, is remarkable in its own way for its contrast between Israel's ancient escape from Egypt "in haste" (cf. Exod. 12:33–34) and the exiles' now imminent, unpanicked rescue from Babylon as they return to their ancestral land. This theme has been in train since Isaiah 40:1–11.

Then suddenly, in 52:13, the lens switches. With the announcement "See, my servant . . . ," we are immediately taken back to the theme initiated in 41:8, and especially in 42:1, which also begins "See, my servant . . ." We noticed in the preceding chapter how this theme winds through chapters 40–55, and its strange interplay between images of an individual and of the people as a whole.[3] There is in this development a growing drumbeat conveying an increasing tendency toward both suffering and the portrayal of an individual. It is a disturbing counterpoint to the story of triumphant Zion-Jerusalem. And 52:13 unmistakably plunges us right back into it. The themes of triumphant Zion and the Suffering Servant are in the end symphonic, and therefore breaks between units in chapters 40–55 are only relative. Nevertheless, in the sudden return to the theme of the servant there is a clear warrant for locating the beginning of a new unit at 52:13.

3. We referred to Isa. 42:1–4; 44:1–2; 45:4; 49:1–6; and 50:4–9, in addition to the present text.

The ending of the unit at 53:12 is marked, like the beginning, by Masoretic punctuation, and in this case it coincides with the chapter division. It is further indicated by the abrupt change of addressee in 54:1 and a resumption of the theme of the salvation of Jerusalem, the "barren one," who is exhorted to sing for joy.

The Structure of Isaiah 53

I have been referring to Isaiah 53 as a poem. We may be accustomed to think of poets in the same bracket as dreamers, not very rooted in reality. However, poetry is one of the dominant forms of expression in the Old Testament. The Old Testament writers evidently believed that poetic forms were often best suited to convey truths about God and the world. So the first observation we should make about the form of our text is precisely that it is a poem. Nor is this merely an incidental point. Form is related to meaning. This will surface in a number of ways in what follows: in the choice of words, in the formation of lines, in the use of images, and in the overall structure. This point is essential to a good reading of Isaiah 53.[4] First, however, we briefly consider the poem's form.

At the heart of the poem, as we have seen, is the image of a suffering individual (53:1–9). So it is striking that this portrayal of a person in the deepest distress opens in 52:13–15 with a declaration of his future exaltation and his powerful impact on rulers. These verses embed in verse 14 an anticipatory description of his suffering, highlighting at the outset the jarring discrepancy between his exaltation and his suffering. At the other end of the poem, the closing verses speak of the vindication and reward that the servant will receive from the LORD (53:10–12).

4. See further below, "Isaiah 53 as Poetry."

These positive notes bookend the core images of suffering and suggest that the composition has a well-thought-out conceptual unity. As we look for the meaning of the servant's suffering, we will be influenced by the sense of purpose expressed by the poem's beginning and end.

The form is notable too because of the changes of speaker and the way in which these changes build up a perspective on the servant. The interplay of voices is unique in the developing story of the servant. The servant himself, who speaks of his own mission and suffering in 50:4–9, is silent now. The opening scene belongs to the LORD, with his declaration that the servant will prosper and be exalted (52:13–15). But at 53:1 a new voice suddenly appears, speaking as "we." These people are unnamed (we will consider more fully who they might be a little later); but it is they who have been witnesses to the servant's distress and who describe his terrible torments. They do so in a retrospective, for they speak in a tone of chastened regret. They had been among those who had despised the servant and thought him accursed by God; but now they know that in truth he had suffered on their behalf and in their place (v. 5). It is at once a confession of guilt and an expression of faith that the LORD has worked their salvation through him (v. 10). The speech of the "we" group gives way again to that of the LORD. This change is not clearly marked, but the LORD is speaking at least from verse 11b. Verses 7–11a could be uttered either by the "we" group or by the poet's own narratorial voice. But the lack of a clear distinction among the voices here has the effect of melding them together; the perspectives of both the "we" group and the poet merge with that of the LORD. (Notice that the analysis of the chapter by speaker in the present paragraph does not map exactly onto the basic division offered in the opening paragraph above.)

Isaiah 53 not only exhibits multiple points of view on the servant but also has an important temporal trajectory, embracing past, present, and future. By this I mean past, present, and future within the world of the text, a set of internal temporal relationships that are not such as can be plotted on a historical timeline.[5] In the past, the servant has experienced violent rejection, apparently by all his peers. In the present, certain people have come to see their former wrong assessment of him. And in the future he will be wonderfully vindicated. The LORD's speech in 52:13–15 enshrines this movement from past to future.

And this feature of the text points to another, namely, the tantalizing questions it raises but does not answer. The identity of the servant himself is unknown, as we have observed. So too is the nature of his suffering and the occasion of it. Who was responsible for it, who are those who once thought him accursed but now know better, and how did they come to see their error? The silence of the servant contributes to this sense of a veil drawn over things. It is a striking feature of the poem's form, inviting a contrast at many points with the Psalms. The psalmists are in no way reticent about voicing their own sufferings at the hands of enemies and articulating their deep fear of being mocked and shamed (e.g., Ps. 25:19–20). The servant, in contrast, allows us to infer his suffering through the words of others. As a poetic device, it is at least as effective as the Psalms in engaging the reader's sympathetic attention.

5. That is to say, the temporal trajectory is a function of the text's poetics. "The world of the text" is a concept in hermeneutics referring to the world that the text invites the reader to imagine. It is distinguished in principle from "the world behind the text," which refers to the historical and social circumstances within which it was written, and from "the world in front of the text," meaning those contexts in which readers try to make sense of it. The concept of these three worlds is used by Richard S. Briggs in *The Lord Is My Shepherd: Psalm 23 for the Life of the Church* in the present series. As Briggs notes (18n31), the concept is generally traced to Paul Ricoeur but is more conveniently and succinctly expressed in Brueggemann, *Cadences of Home*, 59–61.

Yet, in the context of this refusal of the poem to answer our questions clearly, some rather stupendous things are said. Though entirely innocent (53:9), the servant suffered for "our" transgressions, in order to "heal" us (v. 5); he died (as is implied), yet he will "see offspring and prolong his days" (v. 10); and somehow he will "make many righteous" (v. 11). In the context of Old Testament theology, these are extraordinary claims that point the reader beyond the poem into new dimensions of theological reflection.

The form and structure of Isaiah 53 produce a perspective on the servant that is unique, yet which is bound into the flow of the book of Isaiah. Our understanding of the servant is necessarily affected by what we know of him prior to chapter 53. And the poem itself, as we have seen, raises questions in our minds that make us want to read on in Isaiah.

Isaiah 53 as Poetry

I have suggested that the poetic character of Isaiah 53 is not incidental but of its essence. The artistic and imaginative nature of large parts of the Old Testament has been well recognized and much studied in recent decades. Robert Alter's works on both poetry and narrative are important reference points in the sea change that occurred in Old Testament study around 1980, and an avalanche of similar studies has transformed the landscape since.[6] One element in this move was a realization that the truthfulness of a text does not lie completely in unearthing its "historical" meaning. This is true even of texts with a historical narrative, such as the books of Kings. Such texts *do* tell history, but they are not properly understood when read in an attempt to uncover the imagined "real" history behind the text. Rather, the narrative forms are inseparable from

6. Alter, *Art of Biblical Narrative*; Alter, *Art of Biblical Poetry*.

their meaning.[7] Historical study is not rendered irrelevant by this insight and remains an indispensable element in biblical interpretation. But the relation of history to the meaning of texts is now understood in a different way.

I referred above to the "imaginative" nature of large parts of the Old Testament. Here I tread carefully, because there is a danger of being misunderstood. When I say "imaginative" I do not mean fanciful or unreal. On the contrary, I mean that the human imagination is an essential aspect of our God-given capacity to grasp what is really true. Behind this statement lies a certain philosophical story. The thinkers of the Enlightenment made a separation between what they believed could be established by science and reason and what they saw as a poetic or imaginative way of thinking, which was merely decorative and could not contribute to real understanding.[8] Many contemporary thinkers, however, have greater respect for the capacity of imaginative language to speak truthfully about reality. The philosopher Mary Midgley, criticizing the "imperialism" of exclusivistic science, has a chapter tellingly entitled "The Cognitive Role of Poetry."[9] And metaphor too, that close companion of poetic expression, has been found to be indispensable in many spheres of knowledge about the world, including scientific inquiry. Metaphor essentially involves seeing one thing in terms of another, but this simple idea belies its power to create new ways of grasping reality. Metaphor is memorably described by the philosopher Paul Ricoeur as "a category mistake that clears the way to a new vision."[10] It is a "category mistake" because,

---

7. For a classic formulation, see Frei, *Eclipse of Biblical Narrative*.

8. For the scientist Peter Atkins, it is very simple: "While poetry titillates and theology obfuscates, science liberates" (quoted in Cornwell, *Nature's Imagination*, 123).

9. Midgley, *Science and Poetry*, 51–62. See also her *Myths We Live By*, 18–29, 178–80.

10. Ricoeur, *Rule of Metaphor*, 230 (quoted in Gunton, *Actuality of Atonement*, 77).

to take the case of the "Song of the Vineyard" in Isaiah 5:1–7, a nation is not actually a vineyard; yet to conceive of it as such creates new ways of thinking about it in terms of vitality, fruitfulness, vulnerability, flourishing, and failure. Or, to take a modern example, James Lovelock's famous conception of the world as an organism aimed to transform any notion of the world as a mere object, endlessly exploitable, into one that sees the world as living, growing, interactive, and vulnerable. A preexisting concept (the world as an exploitable object) was exposed to a concept taken from a different sphere of knowledge (biology), and so could be viewed in a completely new way. Lovelock's Gaia hypothesis has its detractors, but it undoubtedly fed into the widespread modern perception of the delicate vulnerability of our environment. This example eloquently testifies to the potential purchase of metaphor on the way things really are. Colin Gunton gives a theological slant to this insight: "Because the world is, so to speak, our shape, and we are world-shaped, there is a readiness of the world for our language, a community of world and person which enables the world to come to speech."[11]

The Old Testament's widespread use of poetry and metaphor, therefore, is not merely a matter of aesthetic choice, but testifies to the ways in which the human mind has a handle on reality. The prevalence of metaphor in Isaiah needs no lengthy demonstration. The battered body in Isaiah 1:5–6 is a picture of suffering Israel. The vineyard image in Isaiah 5:1–7 (a common Old Testament trope) recurs with a fresh twist in Isaiah 27:1–6. Israel also appears, variously, as God's children (1:2–4), his servant (41:8), and his witnesses (43:12). The LORD too is depicted in different guises: as a judge in court (3:13–15); as

11. Gunton, *Actuality of Atonement*, 38. He also notes in this regard that the uses of metaphors in scientific inquiry have resulted in demonstrable advances in knowledge (32–33).

Israel's redeemer, a concept drawn from the language of cus-
tomary law (43:14); as her king, an image laden with religious
and political connotations from the ancient Near East (43:15);
as a warrior (42:13); and—perhaps more surprisingly—as a
woman giving birth (42:14). The list could go on. But always
we are being confronted with the need to understand why the
poet/prophet speaks in the ways he does.

The perception that poetry, along with artistic expression
more generally, enables us to grasp profound truths about
ourselves, God, and the world is not confined to the biblical
writers. The human vocation to know God through poetry
and art has yielded wonderful works that have tapped into
this God-given capacity. George Herbert's famous poem "Love
Bade Me Welcome" teaches no new doctrine, yet it gloriously
illuminates both the meaning of Christ's self-giving love and
the timid reluctance of the believer to grasp it fully. Matthias
Grünewald's Isenheim Altarpiece (ca. 1510–15) poignantly
conveys the heavy weight of sin and pain bearing down on the
crucified Christ, yet at the same time, in his upturned fingers,
his love and prayer for the world. The effect of such art is not
to catechize but to arrest and convince and to take the receiver's
apprehension of truth to a new level. In music, the same might
be said of Handel's *Messiah*, Bach's *St. Matthew Passion*, and
the soaring choral flights of Allegri's *Miserere*. These things are
true of poetry, art, and music because of who we are as human
beings. We do not "know" only through our intellects, but
through our whole makeup: body, mind, and spirit. If we have
ever unexpectedly experienced a certain welling up of emotion
caused by a song, a story, or a picture, it may be because we
have encountered some powerful truth in a deep and inexpressible way. Or, put differently, truth has been apprehended by our
imagination.

In his perceptive study of the human imagination, Malcolm Guite points to the telling insight of Samuel Taylor Coleridge, who wrote,

> The IMAGINATION then I consider either as primary, or secondary. The primary IMAGINATION I hold to be the living Power and prime Agent of all human Perception, as a repetition in the finite mind of the eternal act of creation in the infinite I AM. The secondary I consider as an echo of the former, co-existing with the conscious will, yet still as identical with the primary in the *kind* of its agency, and differing only in *degree*, and in the mode of its operation.[12]

This mighty statement locates the faculty of imagination first in the mind of God, who "imagined" the world into existence, and second in the human mind, which is called to discover God's own eternal imagining as its proper way of apprehending the deepest truth about the creation. The point might be understood theologically in terms of God's making human beings in his "image and likeness" (Gen. 1:26–27). God made human beings for the discovery of the world and of himself and gave them every faculty necessary for the task. The imagination is not separate from this task but is entwined with it. Coleridge has a telling phrase about the human imagination: "co-existing with the conscious will." That means it is not elevated above other human faculties, nor does it override them. It is one of the ways that humans know things.[13]

If all this is true of the best of poetry and art and music in general, what does it mean for how we read the poetry and art of the Bible? Are the Psalms and Isaiah 53 of the same order

---

12. Coleridge, *Biographia Literaria*, 304 (quoted in Guite, *Lifting the Veil*, 55).

13. Another well-known phrase expresses something of this idea of a God-given faculty to know, namely, Johannes Kepler's "thinking God's thoughts after him." Kepler had scientific inquiry in mind. But the idea is equally applicable to poetry and art.

as Herbert and Bach? In principle, what is true of language in general is true of the language of the Bible. We have observed that metaphor functions to transform vision. I referred above to the example of James Lovelock's Gaia hypothesis, which has helped many people view the world in a new way. The same process of understanding operates in the poetry of Scripture. In Isaiah 53 we encounter several metaphors. A persecuted individual can be thought of as a lamb led to the slaughter (53:7). But more importantly, major ideas about the world are in play, notably power, success, sacrifice, and justice. If we thought that earthly power was most manifest in great kings, what must we now think when it is exhibited in a destitute and abject human being? When the servant in the poem is said to be made an "offering for sin" (53:10), we will not understand this by determining first of all what kind of offering is meant and then simply equating the servant's fate with that definition. Rather, we will ask, What does it mean for our concept of an "offering for sin" that it is now embodied in the life (and death) of the person at the heart of this poem?

This transformative power of biblical, prophetic poetry has been well recognized as what Walter Brueggemann called the "prophetic imagination."[14] Brueggemann understood this term broadly to refer to a whole view of reality evinced in the Bible, and supremely by the prophets. Scripture offers an imaginative vision for believers to live by. As Daniel Carroll has put it, "Ideally, Christians are shaped and oriented by the unique imaginative understanding of the world offered in the biblical text."[15] This involves, says Garrett Green, "living in the conviction that the world envisioned in the Bible is the real world."[16] And the way to do this is for the Christian imagination to be

14. Brueggemann, *The Prophetic Imagination*.
15. Carroll R., *The Lord Roars*, 17.
16. Green, *Imagining Theology*, 38.

steeped in the language of the Bible, with all its forms of speech, including the poetic.[17]

Isaiah 53 has a special place in comprehending Christ because of its origin in the biblical book of Isaiah and its reception by generations of believers, especially in the New Testament and the Christian church. Yet my interest here is how it operates on the human mind and heart. In this regard, it is in principle no different from other good poetry that has been inspired by faith and worship. (I use "inspired" here in a general sense.)[18] It has been composed by a poet and should be read as such. This is not to detract from its status as a text that points to the deepest truths about existence; on the contrary, it is supremely adapted to do that very thing.

Conclusion

These reflections on Isaiah 53 as poetry support our earlier consideration of its historical and literary matrices. There we were concerned to show that the meaning of the passage cannot be determined with finality by means of historical, philological, or textual investigations. It comes to us irreversibly bound up with the history of its reception and interpretation. Even determining the text of the poem is an interpretive act (or acts), and it has been determined variously by both Jews and Christians in the context of their wrestling with its theological meaning. The

17. This point has been persuasively argued by Brent A. Strawn in *The Old Testament Is Dying*.

18. Obviously, there is poetry and art that takes no cue from religion and may be indifferent or hostile to it. In such cases the relation to what Christians believe to be true is more complicated. Even so, some of what I am saying here about works of the imagination may apply. For example, if I read an atheistic story about human alienation, such as Albert Camus's *The Outsider* (*L'étranger*), I will bring to it my Christian understanding of the reasons for this aspect of the human condition, and the story itself may move me to grasp it in a new way.

quest for the definitive meaning of Isaiah 53, therefore, apart from the web of meanings spun by those who have nurtured it over many generations, is doomed to fail.

The poetic character of the text leads in the same direction. The poem does not set out to give us information, but rather to move us to new and deeper comprehension. It confronts us with a profound human experience that engages our pre-understanding of the possibilities of physical suffering and abandonment, together with callous, self-serving cruelties, and it seeks to stir up empathy. It also holds out avenues for transformation and hope through the power of self-sacrifice and unexpected redemption. In doing so, Isaiah 53 aims to disturb us deeply by dismantling unspoken expectations about the world and turning things upside down. The poetic form serves this aim. At times, the brokenness of the language corresponds to the unfathomability of the experience portrayed.[19] So too the surprising juxtapositions point to an undefeated openness beyond darkness. The one who is humiliated is glorified! How can such things be? The goal of such a text is nothing less than the moral, spiritual, and conceptual regeneration of those who read it. The story of the poem's reception, briefly sketched in the opening section above, is also a story of how people have felt and responded to such challenges.

These considerations may be taken as pointers to what lies in store in a close reading of Isaiah 53. Some of the questions we may want to bring to it will not be answered in the text. Who was this servant? Did he really die and rise again? Was he an individual, or a corporate entity? Who are the "many," and in what way did he make them righteous? Such questions depend on a false premise: that behind the poem lies a factual story that might be reconstructed by careful inquiry. But the

19. For an example, see the comments on Isa. 52:14 in chap. 3 below.

poem's genius is to stir up possible new construals of human existence in relation to God. As readers we are invited first to allow ourselves to be stirred up, and then to follow lines out from the poem to see where they may lead. This is precisely what the first Christians did when they saw that Isaiah 53 could help them plumb the depths of the life, death, and resurrection of Jesus Christ. Their readings are of the kind that David Ford calls "flowerings," expressions of possibilities that lie latent in the text.[20] It is these possibilities that we now set out to explore in the close reading that follows.

---

20. For the expression, see Ford, *Christian Wisdom*, 387. Ford attributes the term to Ricoeur and cites Ricoeur's "The Nuptial Metaphor," 299–300, as its context.

3

Exposition of Isaiah 53

We come now to a close reading of Isaiah 53 (52:13–53:12). In order to do this carefully, we will have to pay attention to the Hebrew text, and sometimes the ancient Greek translation of the Hebrew. However, the aim is to expound the text for the benefit of readers who do not have these languages, in the hope of showing what underlies English translations and why they often vary from one another. So each verse will be given first in transliterated Hebrew, then in English translation. I do not follow any of the standard translations as a rule. In many cases the translator has to choose among several options, so that no translation can convey all the possibilities in a text. But these will emerge, I hope, in the discussion. Mostly, I will adhere to my translation of the text in the BCOT commentary on Isaiah.[1]

Isaiah 52:13–15: The Servant Humiliated—and Exalted!

In these first three verses, the LORD's direct speech gives the authoritative word on the destiny of his servant. In their movement,

1. See McConville, *Isaiah.*

from the servant's exaltation to his stunning effect on the nations via deep suffering, lies a glimpse of the movement in the whole poem.

52:13

hinnēh yaśkîl ʿabdî   yārûm wəniśśāʾ wəgābah məʾōd.[2]
Listen! My servant will succeed.   He will be high and lifted up, and greatly exalted.

This servant is thrust abruptly into the limelight. The little word *hinnēh* typically appears in older translations as "Behold!" Since that word long ago fell out of fashion in modern English, it is common now to substitute it with "See!" or "Look!" But the word is not essentially visual. Rather, it has the rhetorical effect of saying, "Pay attention! I am about to say something important!" The same word heralds the servant's presentation in 42:1, where "Here is my servant" (NIV, NRSV) is a good attempt to get the flavor of it. I have gone for "Listen!" in our text.

The servant is not new to us at this point. As we have seen, the motif can be traced from 41:8. Our question as readers is, What are we now going to learn about this elusive figure? So far we know several things. First, he is closely identified with historic Israel (41:8; 49:3). Second, the LORD's "soul delights" in him, and he has put his spirit on him (42:1). These are emblems of both intimacy and approval. The LORD has attached himself and his reputation to the servant. When he points to him as "my servant," therefore, he makes a declaration of a close affinity; he says something about himself. Third, the servant

---

2. The space between the words *ʿabdî* and *yārûm* represents punctuation marking a pause between phrases in MT. I have adopted this practice in all the transliterations that follow.

has been appointed to an ambitious mission, which is also the LORD's. He is to "establish justice in the earth" and bring his "instruction" to far-flung places (42:1, 4), matters that are close to the LORD's heart. "Justice" (*mišpāṭ*), together with its sister "righteousness" (*ṣədāqâ*), is what the LORD desires above all for Israel (Isa. 5:7).[3] The same qualities are found in the portrayals of ideal kingship in Isaiah 9:6–7 [5–6] and 11:3–5.[4] "Instruction" (Hebrew *tôrâ*) is often rendered "law," which here is not identical with Mosaic law but refers more generally to the LORD's teaching. In Isaiah, the missions of Israel and the servant are one: to extend the LORD's purpose for Israel to all the world. In Isaiah's picture of redeemed Jerusalem, nations shall come as if in pilgrimage to learn from the LORD's "instruction" (2:3); and the servant is called to bring "justice" to the world (42:1, 4). In accordance with this mission, servant-Israel is expressly called to be the LORD's "witnesses" in a watching world, testifying that the LORD alone is God, contrary to the claims of all rivals (43:10; 44:8). The servant's affirmation of the LORD's uniqueness is inseparable from the LORD's desire for justice to be done throughout the world.

This, then, is what we bring to our reading of the poem. But the LORD's commendation of the servant is nuanced differently than in 42:1. No longer is it just "Here is my servant"; the accent falls, rather, on the word immediately after *hinnēh*, namely, *yaśkîl*, translated here as "will succeed." The meaning "succeed," or perhaps "prosper," is one that *yaśkîl* bears in a number of other Old Testament texts.[5] (Whether it is the best sense in this case we shall return to in a moment.) English

---

3. The two qualities are often paired as "justice and righteousness," an expression that articulates the LORD's desire for a society based not just on rule-keeping but on a pervasive love of what is right.

4. In 11:3–4 the concept of justice appears in forms of the verb "to judge" (*šāpaṭ*).

5. For example, it refers to the military successes of Joshua (Josh. 1:7–8) and David (1 Sam. 18:5, 14–15); and see Jer. 10:21. In Hebrew grammar, the verb is a

word order finds it hard to express this. "Listen! Succeed will my servant" would be oddly Yoda-esque. But the point of the LORD's declaration in this case is to focus on the fact that the servant *will succeed*.

What will this "succeeding" look like? It clearly does not carry the connotation that the servant will merely do well for himself. There is no "prosperity theology" in Isaiah 53! *Yaśkîl* is best understood as success in the mission entrusted to him, namely, to bring justice to the nations and to witness to the LORD's beneficent rule in the world. For the servant to succeed means that he will accomplish this task. As we read on, however, it will become clear that there is more to be unfolded about this success than has been fully worked out in the preceding chapters. It will culminate in the servant's "making many righteous" and "bearing their iniquities" (53:11), which will come by a particularly painful route. It will be a kind of success that has hitherto not been seen and that will be achieved quite counterintuitively: an exaltation through humiliation. Our understanding of this success, therefore, will depend on the full picture of the servant's life that is about to unfold.

Now, it may be that the reader is looking at a standard translation of Isaiah 52:13 that does not have either "succeed" or "prosper" at all, but something like "act wisely" (ESV). This is also a meaning that the word *yaśkîl* bears in some Old Testament texts, such as Proverbs 10:19: "One who restrains their lips acts wisely."[6] Such a translation of our text, therefore, is warranted by analogy just as much as the "succeed" translation, and in fact is supported by the ancient Greek version (LXX).[7]

---

hiphil form, which it has in almost all its occurrences. The hiphil of this verb does not have a causative sense, except in a few cases (e.g., Dan. 9:22).

6. The meaning can vary between "act wisely" and "be wise." For the latter, think of Gen. 3:6: "The tree was to be desired to make one wise" (*ləhaśkîl*).

7. LXX has *sunēsei*, "will understand, have insight."

Contextually, too, it finds support from 53:11, which says that the servant will make many righteous "by his knowledge," an Old Testament idea closely akin to that of wisdom (as in Prov. 1:4, where the word *daʿat* appears in a cluster of "wisdom" vocabulary).

Either of these meanings of *yaśkîl* can make good sense in the context.[8] How curious, then, that the poet has chosen to lay stress on a term that is ambiguous! How should a translator or preacher approach this? One temptation to be avoided is to suppose that the word can mean two different things at the same time. Sometimes, in Hebrew as in English, a given word form can mean entirely different things in different contexts. As language users we are generally capable of knowing which meaning suits a given context, and we do not attempt to put distinct meanings together. For example, a "rake" is not a garden tool with promiscuous tendencies! The present case is, admittedly, more difficult than that, since the context does not give an unequivocal nudge either way. This is perhaps a function of that tendency to non-explicitness in the poem that we have already observed.

It may be, alternatively, that the poet has deliberately created an ambiguity. He has made us pause to think: Which meaning applies here? While, linguistically speaking, one cannot simply aggregate a word's possible meanings, poets may create associations of ideas through their choice of words. It would be misguided to say, on the basis of the possible meanings of *yaśkîl*, that wisdom is always part of true success, or that success will always attend wise action. But the poet may intend to make us think about a possible relationship between the two.

---

8. These two meanings cover the vast majority of the verb's occurrences in the Old Testament. In the view of David Clines, "both meanings ["be wise" and "prosper"] are probably combined, since the servant's success springs directly from his knowledge or experience" (*I, He, We, and They*, 14).

It is a dangerous idea because it can easily slip into a "success" theology. But when we understand that the servant's "success" lies in turning people to the LORD and that it comes through humiliation, then one might see a theological connection between true wisdom and the costly, "successful" accomplishment of something profoundly good.

Perhaps a better angle on this is to say that the text in its ambiguity enables a certain theological suggestiveness, which is evident in ways in which it has been interpreted and translated. When LXX picks up from *yaśkîl* the meaning "be wise," it has not simply selected one of the available lexical options, but has adopted it as an important thrust of the text's meaning. In 52:15, LXX employs a form of the same verb that it uses to translate *yaśkîl* in verse 13: *sunēsousin*, "they will understand." It has apparently done this deliberately so as to bracket verses 13–15 with the concept of insight or understanding, and in this way mark it as a leading theme of the servant's portrayal. The motif of "understanding" is present in the Hebrew of verse 15 (*hitbônānû*). So one cannot say that LXX is wrong in its adaptation of the text; it has simply picked out one of the ways in which the text may be read.

The servant will not only succeed in his mission, but now for the first time it is said that he will be high, lifted up, and greatly exalted. This threefold affirmation is a way of expressing a thought in the highest degree. (Recall the seraphim's threefold cry of "Holy" in Isa. 6:3.) It also belongs to the poetic expression of the text. Its rhythmic quality, with the accent falling on the last syllable of each word, is a device by which the form enhances the meaning. The thought of this second half-line is connected to the first in a way that is typical of Hebrew poetry, through an effect known as parallelism (or "seconding"). Often, the relation of the second half-line to the first is one of enhancement: the second carries the thought of the first further or specifies it in some way. In this case, the success of the servant in the first half-line is further specified in terms of his exaltation.

The servant's experience throughout the poem is depicted as thoroughly human, and this must be the basis of all our theological reflection on him. To be exalted, in ordinary human terms, might mean being vindicated or justified in the face of enemies. Psalm 27 is one of many in which the psalmist longs for deliverance from enemies, and he employs the common metaphor of height in order to express this. In 27:5, he declares that the LORD "will lift me high on a rock." Then he goes on: "And now my head shall be lifted up [*yārûm*] above my enemies all around me" (Ps. 27:6 ESV). This is the first and natural reading of what is in store for the servant. That is, as the poem continues, it is clear that he might well have felt that he had enemies. But like the psalmist, he will finally be raised above them and vindicated.

However, what is said of the servant's exaltation goes beyond this common motif. There is something unusually categorical about it. The accumulation of words meaning "high" pushes beyond the ordinary language of triumph over enemies. Most remarkably, it is language that, in Isaiah, is almost exclusively reserved for the LORD (5:16; 6:1; 33:10; 57:15), with one exception for Mount Zion (2:2). Indeed, the exaltation of the LORD alone is one of the great themes of the book. Isaiah 2:9–21 dwells at length on the point; and all three verbs in our text, or closely related terms, occur in that passage. Others may claim to be exalted: the images of mountains and tall trees, high towers and lofty ships, stand for the kind of human arrogance and self-confidence that, in practice, sets itself against God. All such will be duly cut down to size (2:11–17). Kings and empires are chiefly in Isaiah's crosshairs, especially Assyria and Babylon, whose deluded pretensions are mercilessly exposed (10:5–19; 14:12–21). In contrast, the exalted LORD dwells with those who are humble (57:15). How remarkable, then, that the servant should be hailed in these terms! We have noticed already the LORD's delight in him and close identification with him. But here is a new intensity and a surprising twist. There is no suggestion of arrogance on the part of the servant; on the contrary, he neither does nor says anything to exalt himself. And the humiliation that he endures is willingly accepted (53:7). There is, therefore, something very unusual about the servant's exaltation. The Jewish Targum recognized the extraordinary claims made for the servant by adding to his introduction in 52:13a the term *məšîḥā'*, "the anointed one," to "my servant." This is suggestive of a messianic strand within Jewish biblical interpretation at the time. But more importantly, it testifies to the enormous suggestiveness of the text that it opened up such a possibility in an early interpreter's eyes.[9]

Earlier than the Targum, LXX reflected in its own way on the servant's unusual exaltation. Departing from the Hebrew's use of three terms for "be high," it employs only two, one of which is *doxasthēsetai*, "he will be glorified."[10] Instead of relying on the Hebrew poetic pattern and the effect of the height metaphor, it has selected a verb with the strongest theological connotations. The translator knows the importance of the motif of "glory" as a whole in Isaiah, and, apart from the present verse, he employs it twice in verse 14 and once again in 53:2. "Glory" (Hebrew *kābôd*) belongs especially to the LORD in Isaiah.[11] It

---

9. The Aramaic Targum dates to the Christian era, between 70 and 135 CE.

10. LXX has for Isa. 52:13: "Behold, my servant will understand [*sunēsei*] and will be exalted [*hupsōthēsetai*] and will be glorified [*doxasthēsetai*] greatly."

11. The term *tip'ārâ / tip'eret* is also sometimes translated "glory" in Isaiah; but *kābôd* distinctively expresses the LORD's glorious presence.

occurs memorably both in the prophet's dramatic temple vision of the enthroned LORD, attended by heavenly beings who sing of his holiness and glory (Isa. 6:1–3), and in proclamations of his coming in power and bringing salvation (40:5; 60:1–2). The term can be applied to human beings, to refer to their wealth and status. But, when used of the LORD, "glory" is part of the disclosure of his being, along with holiness (6:3), setting him apart from all others.[12] So, in declaring that the servant will be "glorified," the LXX translator apparently wants to convey that there is something extraordinary about his exaltation. In doing so, the translator has picked up what we also noticed in the height metaphor, namely, a close association between the servant and the LORD himself. Catrin H. Williams notes that "the juxtaposition of *hupsoō* [exalt] and *doxazō* [glorify] is a distinctive characteristic of LXX Isaiah," and further that the same verbal pattern is applied to the LORD in Isaiah (5:16; 33:10), indicating "an intentional alignment of God and his servant."[13]

52:14

ka'ăšer šāməmû 'āleykā rabbîm
Just as many were appalled by the sight of you—

kēn mišḥat mē'îš mar'ēhû wətō'ărô mibbənê 'ādām
his appearance was marred beyond that of a man,   his form
     beyond human semblance—

---

12. See also Isa. 3:8; 24:23; 43:7; 58:8. The glory of Zion in 4:2, 5 is a reflection of the LORD's presence there. "Glory" is applied to people or nations in 16:14; 17:4; 21:16, meaning their wealth, beauty, or honor. While the tone of such attributions can be positive (35:2; 60:13), it can also convey ironically a sense of false pretension (10:16; 14:18; 17:3; 22:18).

13. Williams, "Another Look at 'Lifting Up' in the Gospel of John," 62.

After the opening picture of the servant exalted, this sudden change could not be more startling. Here is a human being so disfigured that his appearance is shocking. The raw humanity of the image is stark, yet he has become so badly deformed that he is barely recognizable as a man.

The focus falls first on the shocked reaction of the many who saw him. The verb *šāmǝmû* conveys astonishment verging on horror (as in Jer. 18:16) and is perhaps best rendered "appalled." The thought is introduced with a conjunction, *ka'ăšer*, which can mean "when" or, as here, "just as." This will connect the thought through to verse 15. But before we get there, there is a pause or interruption to let the reader's gaze fall for a moment on the image itself. It is as if the camera zooms in. In form, this second line (v. 14b) begins to develop the first with the word *kēn*, "so, thus." This combination of *ka'ăšer* and *kēn* serves to introduce corresponding statements: "Just as *x*, so *y*." Yet verse 14b reads more like a parenthesis, represented in my translation and several standard ones (e.g., ESV, NJPS, NRSV) by dashes at the end of the first and second lines.

So who is saying this? In verse 13 we were hearing the voice of the Lord, quite directly as it seemed. But the gaze now seems thoroughly earthly. We have moved abruptly from a grand heavenly declaration to a jarring face-to-face encounter. Several perspectives are brought to bear here, in a kind of rush. The voice of the Lord in verse 13 is also the voice of the poet-prophet, who mediates all the speech in the discourse of Isaiah 40–55. We are still hearing the poet at the opening of verse 14. But then, surprisingly, we find that the speaker is addressing the servant: "as many were appalled by the sight of *you*." The unexpectedness of this is registered by those standard translations that substitute "him" for "you" here (e.g., RSV,

NRSV, NIV). Some ancient readers did the same,[14] but MT has the most important ancient texts (the Qumran Isaiah scroll [1QIsaᵃ] and LXX) on its side, so it is more likely that "you" was changed to "him" by puzzled readers than it is that "him" was changed to "you." (A switch from second to third person for rhetorical effect is found in a number of other poetic texts in Isaiah.)[15]

The poet therefore fleetingly addresses the servant directly. In doing so, he pulls others alongside him into his gaze; these are the "many," unnamed and unnumbered, who looked at the servant and were appalled. It is a dramatic moment, too intense to be sustained, and registered in the broken syntax that we have already noticed. With this literary effect, it is as if the poet and other onlookers pull away, and the servant's isolation is vividly portrayed. The discourse returns immediately to the third person, to describe what it was about the servant that had appalled so many.

He was, we are told, so disfigured and deformed that he scarcely looked like a human being. The second line in verse 14 has two parts, each with a word related to "seeing," *mar'ēhû* and *tō'ărô*, translated here as "appearance" and "form."[16] Each of these in turn is paired with a word for "man" or "human being" (*'îš* and *'ādām*). So there is a strong focus on the visual impact made by the servant, which almost defies description. The word that carries the weight of this, here translated "marred," is *mišḥat*, which governs both parts of the line. Oddly, this noun occurs only here in the Old Testament and may be a further instance of the poet's use of language that gives pause for thought. It is almost certainly related to the verbal root *šḥt*, meaning "to corrupt" or "be corrupted," hence

---

14. Syriac, Targum, and some medieval Hebrew manuscripts.
15. E.g., Isa. 42:20; 45:21; 61:7.
16. These nouns are related formally to the verb *rā'â*, "to see."

its common translation as "marred" or "disfigured."[17] Yet, in line with the poet's love of suggestive language, the form bears a resemblance to a quite different word, *māšaḥ*, "anoint." This ambiguity is highlighted by the Qumran Isaiah scroll, which, by the addition of a single letter, has the form *mšḥtî*, possibly to be read *māšaḥtî*, "I anointed."[18] It is debatable whether 1QIsa^a actually means this, or whether it has simply used a variant of a form meaning "mar" or "corrupt."[19] It is hard to make good sense of the reading "I anointed," and it may be that the Qumran scribe has only hinted at the meaning "anoint," with its messianic connotations. But this connotation is in line with the pervasive idea in Isaiah 40–55 of the servant as one called by the LORD to a special work.

We may note at this point that LXX has negotiated the word *mišḥat* in its own way, with the verb *adoxēsei*: "he was held in low esteem." This verb is related to *doxa*, "glory," which as we have indicated is a key motif of LXX in Isaiah 52:13–53:12. The servant, who is declared to be "glorified" in verse 13 (*doxasthēsetai*), is now treated as inglorious. The contrast is not without force, in terms of LXX's rhetoric. As in the Great Isaiah Scroll, the unusual and challenging form of *mišḥat* has sparked theological reflection, and here too it is in line with a feature of the servant's portrayal, in this case his close and intimate association with the LORD himself.

While these ancient readers have given stimuli to theological reflection in the text, it is important for us not to lose the starkness of the poet's vision. He has touched a nerve in the reader,

---

17. The verb occurs most frequently in the hiphil, *hišḥît*, "to ruin," and also in the niphal, *nišḥāt*, "to be marred or ruined."

18. The Qumran scroll lacks the vowel pointing of MT. The form *māšaḥtî* supplies vowels according to the reading "I anointed." The consonantal text frequently allows quite different construals of its forms, depending on which vowels are supplied by the reader.

19. This point is discussed in detail by Koole, *Isaiah* III/2, 268–70.

the instinctive recoil from terrible human suffering manifest in a person's appearance. We cannot have a photographic image of what the servant looked like, nor do we know what has caused his disfigurement. And it is no doubt part of the effectiveness of the image that it is left to the reader's imagination. (As in a horror movie, the deepest emotions are awakened by what is not seen, but only suggested.) Even so, the vision is laid before us unsparingly, at the outset of the servant's portrayal in chapter 53. In the developing story of the servant in Isaiah 40–55, this is a new and climactic intensification. It seems we are meant to resist the instinct to recoil. If we do not face up to the repugnant image, we risk losing the impact of the poem as a whole.

The point has an obvious relevance to a reading of Isaiah 53 with the suffering of Christ in mind. The Gospels make it clear that he endured immense physical agony in his last days, both in the tortures inflicted on him before his execution and on the cross itself. The cross was used by the Romans not only as a means of execution but as a public display of humiliation and an assertion of total power over people's lives. The brutality of it was intended not only to cause pain but to humiliate the victim in the highest degree. It was an extreme attack on the person's very humanity, the calculated denaturing of a human being, the brutal exposure of one thus dehumanized, turned into nonhuman, expelled from human society, stripped of every right to the name and dignity of human. Crucifixion was much more than merely getting rid of an awkward enemy; it aimed to extinguish any claim to a way of being human that did not conform to the tyrant's version of reality. As such, it was a perversion of the truly human.

In Christian spirituality, it is perhaps because the cross is a shocking corruption of what is true and good in humanity that the contemplation of it has played such an important part over the centuries.[20]

52:15

kēn yazzeh gôyim rabbîm   ʿālāyw yiqpəṣû məlākîm pîhem
so he will startle many nations;   kings will be dumbstruck because of him.

kî ʾăšer lōʾ-suppar lāhem rāʾû   waʾăšer lōʾ-šāmʿû hitbônānû
For they will have seen something previously untold to them,
and will have understood a thing they had never heard.

After the pause in verse 14b, the train of thought continues. Like verse 14b, verse 15 opens with *kēn*, "so, thus," connecting back to "just as" (*kaʾăšer*) in verse 14a. But now, instead of a zooming-in effect, there is a logical development. The sense of verses 14–15, in a nutshell, is: Just as many were appalled at the servant (he was so disfigured), so he will dumbfound kings and nations.

The poet does not put things in nutshells, however. Once again, the very first word (after *kēn*) gives cause to pause. In texts dealing with sacrificial rituals, *yazzeh* is usually translated "sprinkle."[21] The unexpectedness of this idea in 52:15, however, has prompted interpreters to look for possible alternative meanings. The context creates an expectation of something like "astonish" because of verse 14a ("many were appalled") and the second half-line of verse 15: "kings will be dumbstruck." And we have been given a reason for such strong reactions in the

---

20. For further reflection on this, see chap. 4, below.
21. The word *yazzeh* is a hiphil form of *nzh*. It occurs in texts concerning a variety of rituals around the altar in the tabernacle, mainly involving the sprinkling of blood (e.g., Lev. 4:6, 17), but also oil or water (Lev. 14:16; Num. 8:7).

servant's terrible appearance. The motivation to find a meaning more fitting to the context is ancient, as LXX's *thaumasontai*, "will be astonished," attests.[22] Modern interpreters suggest either emending the verb or seeking alternative meanings of *yazzeh*, the most common proposal being "to leap," hence our translation "startle."[23]

But perhaps the poet is teasing us again. Not for the first time, he has given us a word that can be taken in either of two ways, forcing us to choose, when perhaps the choice necessarily involves some loss. (He did not write with translators in mind!) We may well opt for "startle," yet we cannot move on without having to consider whether the meaning "sprinkle" might make sense. Since the action of sprinkling in its typical Old Testament contexts implies purification, might the point be that the servant will have a purifying or cleansing effect on nations? There is some warrant for this in the previously disclosed mission of the servant to be a witness to the LORD and to bring his justice to the ends of the earth. And this warrant is strengthened when we reread verse 15 as part of the full picture in Isaiah 53, in which the servant will "make many righteous," be "wounded for our transgressions," and "bear their iniquities" (53:5, 11). There are hints in this language of a sacrificial aspect to the servant's sufferings, which we shall explore further in due course.

Rather than pretend that we can choose decisively between translations of *yazzeh* in our verse, therefore, it is better to ask how far each of them illuminates themes in the poem. Arguably,

22. It is not clear what authority LXX had for this rendering. 1QIsa^a is as MT, and the Latin Vg. has *asperget*, meaning "will sprinkle."

23. An emendation of *yazzeh* to *yirgəzû*, "they will tremble, be agitated," is sometimes proposed. The meaning "leap, be startled" for *yazzeh* is based, perhaps tenuously, on a similar-looking Arabic verb meaning "leap up" and has been espoused by numerous commentators, as well as RSV, NRSV, and JPS/NJPS.

each translation does help us read the poem carefully. The idea that the servant "startles" nations chimes with the following half-line, in which he will strike kings dumb (about which more in a moment). The idea that he "sprinkles" them alerts us to the fact that this deep impact on rulers and nations is not a matter of naked power, but is transformative in a profound and surprising way. As we ponder this, we do well to recall that we read the text in fellowship with the many who have gone before us, as well as the many who continue to read alongside us. And we learn with and from them that both interpretations can be insightful guides. As with the "succeeds/is wise" dilemma in verse 13, we do not aggregate the separate meanings of the verb into some inclusive higher concept; rather, we admire the poet's ingenuity in prodding us into searching reflection on his meaning.

This deep impact of the servant will be felt by "many na-tions." This recurrence of "many" as a motif in these lines is significant. There is a fullness in "many" that speaks of God's generosity. It is redolent of the ancient promise to Abraham that his descendants would be as numerous as the stars (Gen. 15:5), that he would be the ancestor of a throng of nations (17:5), and that kings and nations would come from him (17:6). The assurance that "many" will come to know and worship the LORD is a motif in the Psalms (Ps. 40:3 [4]). In Isaiah 52:14, the "many" are unidentified and are best taken to refer to other Israelites, in line with the servant's mission to Jacob-Israel in 49:6. Now the "many" are specified as nations, in an unmistak-able widening of the scope. This also has a precedent in 49:6, with its deliberate progression from the servant's mission to restore Jacob-Israel to his being given as a "light to the na-tions." The servant's significance is set in a wide international context. The point is developed in the next half-line in 52:15:

"kings will be dumbstruck because of him," or more exactly, they will "shut their mouths because of him." The implication is that whatever the servant has become or done will change the course of human history.

This development stretches the imagination in a new way. While it was possible to think of a disfigured person causing embarrassment and revulsion to individuals who encountered him, it is difficult to carry this image over to a geopolitical context. In what way could the manifest sufferings of an individual affect the world of international relations? The servant's role in world affairs is not new at this point in Isaiah, as we have seen above.[24] He stands alongside the Persian king Cyrus, two figures each with a role in the purpose of the LORD for the salvation of Israel. Cyrus is charged with a political and military mission: to restore Judean exiles to their land and to rebuild the ruins of Jerusalem (44:24–45:7). The role of the servant of the LORD, understood as Jacob-Israel, is to function as "a witness" to the work of the LORD in the eyes of the nations (41:8; 43:8–10). There is no simple divide here between political and religious spheres, nor between the servant as an individual and as a corporate entity.

This is pointedly illustrated by the saying in 49:7, the immediate sequel to the servant passage in 49:6, concerning the servant as "a light to the nations." Here servant-Israel is depicted as, first, "deeply despised," or "despised in his life/soul" (*libzōh nepeš*), then as "abhorred by the nation."[25] The word "abhorred" is a strong term of reprobation (*mətāʿēb*); "nation" is singular (*gôy*), and therefore the line hints at the radical

24. See the introduction and the subsection "The Book of Isaiah" under "Isaiah 53 in Its Contexts."

25. The phrase *mətāʿēb gôy* is strictly "one despising a nation." A passive sense seems to be called for by the context and is supported by 1QIsaᵃ in the case of "despised" (*libzûy* rather than *libzōh*), and LXX in the case of "abhorred" (*bdelussomenon*, suggesting the pual participle [*li*]*mtōʿāb* for MT piel [*li*]*mtāʿēb*).

rejection of an individual by the nation of Israel. (This singular is often rendered as a plural [NJPS, NRSV], taking the singular as representative of the generality, perhaps to make a smoother parallel with "servant of rulers.") "servant of rulers" ironically depicts servant-Israel (the nation) as enslaved by powerful enemies and humiliated in the eyes of the world because of its defeat and exile, the destruction of its temple and ruin of its land.

Abruptly, the tone changes from reprobation to vindication: "Kings will see you and rise to their feet, princes, and they will bow down" (49:7). The contrast between humiliation and exaltation is strikingly similar to the contrast in 52:13–15. Kings did not rise to their feet for anybody, nor did princes bow down.[26] It is a bold image, and no doubt hyperbolic. It can only be occasioned by an exceptional work of the LORD, as the last phrase in 49:7 makes clear. And that work is the transformation of a broken people in the restoration of exiles to Jerusalem and the reestablishment of the nation there.

Isaiah 49:7, together with the preceding verses 1–6, highlights the mobility of concept between the suffering individual and the suffering nation. And this helps toward an understanding of 52:15. That kings should "be dumbstruck" because of the servant is also a bold image. Kings spoke and commanded. But here they are silenced. And the best explanation of this is that they are astonished by the wretched condition to which Jerusalem and Judah were reduced and by their transformation.

The vindication of Jerusalem is not expressed in 52:15a in the way that it is in 49:7. If we infer that it was part of what stunned the kings into silence, we do so in the light of the declaration in 52:13 that the LORD's servant would be exalted. And the

---

26. There is no material difference between "kings" and "princes" here. The two terms echo each other in poetic parallelism.

second half of verse 15 also implies that there was something extraordinary about what they were seeing.

The last line (v. 15b) offers an explanation for the kings' astonished silence. The verbs are in the Hebrew perfect tense, which normally indicates the past, but here the past is in relation to their still future seeing of the servant, hence the "future perfect": "They will have seen something previously untold to them, and will have understood a thing they had never heard." The kings recognize in what they see and hear something qualitatively different from anything they have witnessed before: something that no messenger has ever reported, something they have never previously heard. We know that what they have seen is what has happened to the servant. But their perception of it is now raised above the ordinary observation of historical events.

In the book of Isaiah, the language of seeing, hearing, and understanding is heavily loaded. When the kings are said to see, hear, and understand something new, the readers' antennae remind them of that most puzzling saying of the LORD in Isaiah 6:9–10, in his commission to Isaiah the prophet:

> And [the LORD] said: "Go and say to this people:
>
>> 'Keep on hearing, but you will not understand!
>> Keep on seeing, but you will not attain knowledge.'
>> Make the minds of this people thick, their ears dull and their
>>> eyes blind,
>> lest they see with their eyes, hear with their ears, and
>>> understand with their minds,
>> lest they repent and are healed!"

The book of Isaiah unfolds in the wake of this strange charge.[27] It is the foundation of the book's overarching concept of a

---

27. The forms *wəʾal-tābînû* and *wəʾal-tēdāʿû* are strictly negative imperatives: "do not understand . . . do not attain knowledge!" They are ironic in tone, somewhat

movement from judgment to salvation, which is heralded by the great cry of "Comfort!" in 40:1–2. For the progression from judgment to salvation is at the same time a progression from incomprehension to comprehension. The leitmotif of seeing, hearing, and understanding runs through this story. The idea of the blind seeing and the deaf hearing is, in one sense, a sign of the future renewal of all things, as in 29:18 and 35:5. But it is also tightly bound up with the themes of sin and salvation. The dulling of the senses stands for a deep incomprehension of the way things truly are. This amounts to a failure to grasp the reality of God and his ways in the world. Incomprehension is a facet of the fundamental rejection of God. When the mind is darkened, all manner of evil can seem wise, a perversion that is exposed in a passage like 29:13–16.

The pathway that leads out of darkness into light is neither neat nor smooth, however. While 40:1–2 appears to announce a categorically new phase in Israel's life, servant-Israel is still found to be deaf and blind in 42:18–20. The movement out of incomprehension is evidently always dependent on the LORD's people rising to the challenge, and this accounts for the hortatory tone that is adopted throughout chapters 40–55, notably in the rhetorical gambit of 43:8–10:

> Bring out the people that is blind though having eyes,
> that is deaf, though having ears.

---

like "However much I tell you, you will never learn." They are, in effect, not predictions but moral exhortations. It is best, therefore, not to take these verses as a basis for a philosophical theology of predestination. Even so, they form part of the prophetic book's rationale for the people of Israel's two hundred years of savage attack, first from Assyria, then Babylon. In spite of all that horror, which included the loss of the northern kingdom of Israel as well as the destruction of Solomon's temple and the ruin of Judah, the LORD has not finally abandoned his people. This is how the Gospels and Acts, in their different ways, interpret this difficult text, naturally finding in Jesus the decisive confirmation of the prophetic promise. See Matt. 13:14–15; Mark 4:12; John 12:39–41; Acts 28:26–28.

> All the nations have gathered together,
>> the peoples are assembling.[28]
> Who among them can declare this?
>> Who can proclaim to us the former things?
> Let them bring witnesses to show they are right.
>> Let them listen, and speak the truth.
> You are my witnesses, says the LORD,
>> my servant whom I have chosen,
> so that you may know and trust me,
>> and understand that I am he.

Here the servant-people of Israel are called to be witnesses to the right of the LORD alone to be known as God. Yet these witnesses are still "blind" and "deaf" (v. 8), an impossibility for true witnesses. This prophetic speech is therefore a clarion call to the servant-people themselves to wake up to true understanding so that they can be who they really are.

It is in the midst of this scenario that the enlightening of kings in 52:15b is suddenly declared. In a story in which servant-Israel seems to be forever hesitant to embrace its destiny to bring "light to the nations," kings are given to see, hear, and understand. This vision is best understood as the disclosure of an ultimate reality, a foretaste of a time when kings and rulers will grasp the true significance of what God has done through Israel: how by its humiliation and rejection by all who saw it, it became the means of God's disclosure of himself in the world. To see what they had not previously seen, therefore, is not a description of anything within the world of ordinary politics; it is a spiritual insight, heralding a revolution in the very order of things.

The apostle Paul cites this text in support of his mission to bring the gospel of Christ to the Gentiles. For him, this is what

---

28. "Have gathered . . . are assembling": the tense of the first verb, *niqbəṣû*, is perfect ("they have gathered"), while the second, *wəyēʾāsəpû*, is simple waw followed by imperfect. The sequence suggests a continuous gathering.

is meant ultimately by coming to see and understand (Rom. 15:18–21, esp. 21). He also pursues the theme in respect of kings and rulers, however, who are still in incomprehension of the wisdom of God. Christ crucified is "a stumbling block to Jews and foolishness to Gentiles" (1 Cor. 1:23 NRSV). God's wisdom is diametrically opposed to the "wisdom of this age," and the "rulers of this age" do not understand it (1 Cor. 2:6–8 NRSV). Understanding is given by the Spirit of God to those who know that God's wisdom is manifest in the life, death, and resurrection of Jesus Christ (2:10–13). And when Paul explains these things, his language touches intriguingly on our text in Isaiah: "'What no eye has seen, nor ear heard, nor the human heart conceived . . .'—these things God has revealed to us through the Spirit" (1 Cor. 2:9–10 NRSV).

Paul's allusion is difficult to pin down exactly. It is closest to Isaiah 64:4 (64:3 LXX), which does not have only rulers in its sights. While in Paul it is not limited to rulers either, it is nevertheless prompted by his line of thought on rulers and so has an echo of Isaiah 52:15b. The echo is one of contrast, however, for in Isaiah the kings are said to see and understand, whereas in Paul they are unable to do so. It should be said that there is no exact correspondence between the "kings" in Isaiah and the "rulers of this age" in Paul, for the latter probably includes all kinds of earthly, and even unearthly, powers.[29] Even so, when the text in Isaiah is read in the light of Paul, it strengthens our point that the kings' understanding of what they see in the servant is a glimpse into something that transcends whatever historical context one might find for

---

29. New Testament scholars debate whether the "rulers" (*archontes*) in 1 Cor. 2:6–8 are human authorities or something greater than the merely human, whether demonic or sociopolitical. For an account, see Thiselton, *First Epistle to the Corinthians*, 233–39. Thiselton sees the "rulers of this world order" (his translation) as "socio-political powers in a structural collectivity that transcends given human individuals" (238).

it. It looks beyond the immediate conflicts of the prophet's day, and even Paul's, to a time when, at the name of Jesus, "every knee should bend, in heaven and on earth and under the earth" (Phil. 2:10 NRSV).

Afterthought on 52:13–15

The three verses at the end of Isaiah 52 are a kind of overture to the remainder of the poem in chapter 53. They encompass some of the essential themes and paradoxes in the chapter. The question "Who is the servant?" finds no unambiguous answer. His portrayal in chapters 40–50 invites perceptions of both the chosen people Jacob-Israel and a prophetic individual; he is both Israel and distinct from it. The poetics of chapter 53 will lead the imagination predominantly toward the individual. But 52:13–15 does not entirely resolve the question. There is at no point an announcement that the figure in 52:13 is now distinct from the one introduced in 41:8. The imagery of 52:14 invites the contemplation of a human being, a suffering, isolated figure. But verse 15 shifts attention back to the international stage on which the drama of Jacob-Israel has been playing out. As readers, we are bound to ask how these two perceptions of the servant relate to each other. And as we move into chapter 53, the poet will not let us forget this question.

The second major theme is the relationship between the servant's exaltation and his humiliation. This extraordinary paradox is a vital ingredient in the servant's portrayal throughout chapter 53 and a harbinger of the Johannine mystery of Christ's exaltation on the cross. The idea of the servant's exaltation has a historical contact point in the remarkable restoration of exiles to Jerusalem and the unexpected reversal of imperial policy that not only allowed the exiles to return but furnished the means for the rebuilding of city and temple. But it cannot be confined to this. The paradox of humiliation and exaltation leads on toward an even more profound synthesis.

The timescale is correspondingly elusive. The servant's story must be imagined first of all in the context of Judah under Babylon and Persia. But the text slides easily from past to future. Many *were astonished* at the servant; but he *will succeed*, and kings *will see*. As we have noticed, the "astonishment" of kings was still a powerful factor in the time of the apostle Paul; and their comprehension of the ways of God remains incomplete. The servant's mission is worked out across the ages, reaching beyond the resurrection of Christ and into an indeterminate future. As we think of these opening verses of our text in relation to the work of Christ, we may be reminded of the declaration of the mystery of faith, according to a time-honored liturgy:

> Christ has died,
> Christ is risen,
> Christ will come again![30]

30. Compare the view expressed by Franz Delitzsch in his great commentary on Isaiah nearly two centuries ago:

> When Isaiah sang his dying song on the border line of the reigns of Hezekiah and Manasseh, all the coming sufferings of his people appeared to be concentrated in the one view of the captivity in Babylon. And it was in the midst of this period of suffering, which formed the extreme limit of his range of vision, that he saw the redemption of Israel beginning to appear. He saw the servant of Jehovah working among the captives, just as at His coming He actually did appear in the midst of His people, when they were in bondage to the imperial power of the world; he also saw the Servant of Jehovah passing through death to glory, and Israel ascending with Him, as in fact the ascension of Jesus was the completion of the redemption of Israel. . . . It is only the coming of Christ in glory which will fully realize what was not yet realized when He entered into glory after the sufferings of death. (Delitzsch, *Prophecies of Isaiah*, 304 and note)

In lines omitted from the cited passage, Delitzsch explains that the full redemption of Israel in the period of the Babylonian exile could not be realized because of "the unbelief of the great mass of Israel," and therefore that "this redemption was at first merely the spiritual redemption of believers out of the nation"; the full redemption of Israel would come only after the return of Christ in glory.

Isaiah 53:1–3: A Picture of Human Torment

The servant draws no attention to himself. He has been brought into our field of vision by others: the LORD has declared that he will be exalted; "many" were appalled at the sight of him; kings and nations will be astonished by him; and the poet conducts the choir of voices, affirming that what the kings and nations have not heard before, they shall understand (52:13–15). Now a new voice is heard, a plural voice, speaking as "we." They speak without fanfare or introduction, but are suddenly on stage and hold the floor at least until verse 6. They are unnamed, but they know the servant well. It is sometimes thought that they are the "many," or perhaps the "kings," in 52:13–15. There is, indeed, a connection between 52:15 and 53:1 in the motif of "hearing," and also in the concept of a dawning understanding where there had been none before. (This emerges strongly in 53:1–6.) Yet there is no necessary connection between the figures in 52:13–15 and these new speakers. Their anonymity is another of those teasing silences of Isaiah 53. Their abrupt intrusion into the discourse is meant to arrest our attention, to paint another hue into the emerging picture.

Readers of Isaiah know too that an unidentified "we" voice has spoken at other times in the book, always with the effect of placing an event under scrutiny from a vantage point outside it. The first instance is in 1:9, where a graphic image of a body battered and bruised, perhaps a victim of war (1:5–6), is contemplated in retrospect, again by an anonymous "we," who have come to see that a terrible experience of Israel had its place in God's purpose ultimately to save. In Isaiah 40–55, such a voice has been met in 40:8; 42:24; and 47:4, always in a tone of confession or penitence. These are "knowing" utterances, aligned with the prophetic or editorial perspective of the whole book. The present passage differs from them in the sense that the speech is relatively extensive and tells a kind of story. The nearest analogy in Isaiah is 63:16–19, in which a group within Israel laments that it has been marginalized and oppressed. Yet this too differs from 53:1–6, because the sufferer in our text does not speak for himself.

Our best guess is simply to suppose that the speakers (or one of them who speaks on their behalf) are a group within the community of returned exiles and other inhabitants of Jerusalem and Judah who have come to recognize that they have been guilty of failing to understand the real character of the servant figure and of the terrible things he endured. This means that the depiction of people's abhorrence at his appearance is entwined with its interpretation. The speakers were among those who could not bear to see him (53:2b, 3b). Only in retrospect, from their new, chastened perspective, are they able, as it were, to look him squarely in the face. This point is vital for an understanding of the second half of the book of Isaiah. The exile has ended, and the LORD has "comforted" his people (40:1–2). But members of the community still face existential decisions about the true nature of servant-Israel and how they will take their place within it. What changed the minds of this confessing group is one of the poem's intriguing silences, which we will consider further in a moment.

Finally, regarding the rhetorical and poetic effect of the "we" voice, it powerfully arrests *us*, the readers. Who originally stood behind these verses, we cannot know. But neither can we avoid the sense that their confession intends to draw us, who read it centuries later, into a true appraisal of the servant and an assent to who he really was.

53:1

mî he'ĕmîn lišmuʿātēnû   ûzərôaʿ yhwh ʿal-mî niglātâ

> Who has believed what we have heard? And to whom has
> the arm of the LORD been revealed?

The opening question, "Who has believed?" is an utterance of amazement. There is in it a sense that what the faithful group have come to understand strains credulity. The Greek LXX turns it into a prayer, prefixing an address to the LORD (*kurie*). In doing so, it recognizes that the servant's impact exceeds ordinary expectations.

While the question is at one level the expression of the believers' experience, it is in the rhetoric of the poem a challenge to anyone who will listen. The faithful group wants others to see what they have come to see. As "belief," it will be a matter of insight and thus faith and trust. This is a major theme of Isaiah 40–55. Will the restored community believe that the LORD really can do what he says he can do, in the face of the claims of the visibly powerful (empires and their gods) to be the controllers of events and destinies? And in a killer twist, will they believe that he can do it through the humiliation of the servant?

The phrase "what we have heard" is tantalizing. In the Hebrew, it is just one word, *lišmuʿātēnû*, which, put very woodenly, is "our heard thing." This is ambiguous: Does it mean the thing that we have heard, or the thing that we are passing on to others to hear? Both of these are represented in standard translations (e.g., "what we have heard," NRSV; "our message," NIV). The ambiguity perhaps does not need to be resolved. What the believers have come to understand is something that has been given to the hearing. We have noticed the importance of the "hearing" motif in Isaiah 52:15, where it was said of kings and nations that their "hearing," together with their "seeing," was the gateway to their new and profound understanding. The believers describe their new grasp of who the servant really was as something they have "heard." They do not say more about the nature of their experience. But we know that true hearing is profoundly spiritual, often running against the grain of ordinary human calculation.

This point is vividly clear when we compare 28:9–13, a little cameo of willful unbelief, and especially verse 9b, which has a striking echo of our text: "to whom would he . . . explain what has been heard [*šəmûʿâ*]?" With its rhetorical question and its use of the same noun, *šəmûʿâ*, there is an unmistakable echo between the texts. It is all the sharper because the question in 28:9 is uttered in a tone of mockery by the very people whom the prophet is condemning for unbelief. These errant leaders of the community are lampooning the prophet for imagining that he knows better than they do what has been handed down as true. The last word in both texts, however, is with the prophet, who knows that hearing and understanding is a matter of spiritual insight. The author of John's Gospel knew this too, when he cited Isaiah 53:1 to illustrate unbelief in his own generation and paired it with Isaiah 6:9–10, that great text of willful refusal to believe (John 12:38–40). The apostle Paul also cites our passage as a text of unbelief but turns it to the positive message that "faith comes from hearing," adding that hearing is "through the word of Christ" (Rom. 10:16–17 ESV). Like John, Paul shows his command of the context in Isaiah, since in the preceding verse (10:15) he had just cited Isaiah 52:7: "How beautiful are the feet of those who bring good news!" (NRSV). In this way he too brings the topic of faith and hearing into the context of the gospel of Christ.[31]

The rhetorical question in Isaiah 53:1a is echoed by another in verse 1b: "And to whom has the arm of the LORD been re-

---

31. From Isa. 52:7, Paul cites the phrase in Greek: *tōn euangelizomenōn ta agatha*, "those who bring good news of good things" (Rom. 10:15); then in 10:16 he writes, "But not all have obeyed the *gospel* [*tō euangeliō*]."

vealed?"[32] The "arm of the LORD" is a common anthropomorphism, much used in the songs of Israel to celebrate his great power in creation and in history (e.g., Pss. 44:3 [4]; 77:15 [16]; 89:10 [11]). By his "mighty arm" he had stilled the powers of chaos at the creation, and by it he rescued Israel from slavery in Egypt, in the earliest days of their formation as his covenant people (Deut. 4:34). By it too he could even bring judgment against them when they had broken the covenant (Jer. 21:5). The LORD's overwhelming power in both nature and history was an essential article of Israel's faith in him as the one God, and it is central to the theological mission of Isaiah 40–55 (e.g., Isa. 40:21–23). In the run-up to the present text, the motif has occurred several times. In 48:14 the LORD's arm is turned against the Babylonians, as he acts to deliver his people from their oppression. It appears again in Isaiah 51:5, 9–11, with a reference to his ordering power in creation (vv. 9–10), which undergirds his purpose to redeem the exiles, bringing them to Zion with singing and everlasting joy (v. 11). And in 52:10, the LORD's powerful salvation is described as a baring of his "holy arm" before the eyes of the whole world. This is the broad context in which we encounter the Suffering Servant.

And so we are confronted once more with the profound paradox of the servant. For this revelation of the "arm of the LORD" is placed on a par with belief in "what we have heard." In the present verse it makes a surprising contrast with the overwhelming, visible power implied in the "arm" texts that

---

32. The phrasing of the question, *ʿal mî niglātâ*, is unusual because of the preposition *ʿal* rather than the expected *ʾel mî*, "to whom." It could be rendered "Upon whom has the arm of the LORD been revealed?," implying that the interrogative *mî* ("who, whom") refers to the servant. The sense would be: Can the salvation of the LORD have been accomplished by what has been done to this man? LXX translates the line as if it had *ʾel*, "to." Among commentators, Goldingay takes *ʿal* as "upon" (*Message of Isaiah 40–55*, 495–96). There is not much at stake for the meaning of the phrase.

we have just noticed. This mighty act of God is not, it seems, a dramatic sign that no one could fail to observe. Rather, it is revealed; and the question "to whom?" makes it clear that, like the thing that is heard, it is revealed to faith. What, then, is this mighty act that is known only by revelation? The answer is in the verses that follow. The mighty act of God, counterintuitively, will consist, somehow, in the suffering figure at the heart of our text. The exhilarating image of the joyful return to Zion is mediated through the humiliation of the servant.

53:2

wayya'al kayyônēq ləpānāyw   wəkaššōreš mē'ereṣ ṣiyyâ

He grew up like a green shoot before him,   like a root out of arid ground.

lō'-tō'ar lô wəlō' hādār wənir'ēhû   wəlō'-mar'eh wənehmədēhû

He had no beauty or noble aspect that we should look at him;   nothing in his appearance that we should find him attractive.

The unattractive appearance of the servant was adumbrated in 52:14, and now it is elaborated (53:2–3). In verse 1, we were prepared for something extraordinary, and in these verses the nature of it begins to be unfolded.

The verse opens with the unobtrusively simple "he grew up before him." Neither "he" nor "him" is identified. Because we have already been reading since 52:13, we infer that "he" is the servant. The phrase "before him" arrests our attention. We might have expected "before us," since the "we" are otherwise the viewing agents throughout verses 2–3. That the one called "him" is the LORD can be assumed from the mention of the LORD in verse 1. The reticence of the phrase gives the impression that something is about to be unfolded that has not yet been fully disclosed. The chief effect of the line, however, is that both the servant and the LORD are placed at the heart of the story. While there is a strong emphasis in this and the following verses on the servant as seen by human beings, this line sets down a marker: the real significance of the servant's life hangs on how it is seen by God.[33]

When a person is said to be, or live, or stand "before the LORD," it usually means that they are somehow in his favor (e.g., Gen. 17:18; 27:7; 1 Kings 17:1; Jer. 30:20). The servant is said to have "come up" (*wayya'al*) before him. In what way has he "come up"? One standard translation (JPS) takes it as "shot up," conforming to the botanical image in the rest of verse 2a. However, perhaps because the word *yônēq*, "shoot," can also mean "child," most translators render *wayya'al* as "grew up," conveying that the eye of the LORD was on the servant over time. This may fit more comfortably with the common usage of "before the LORD"; verses 2–3 generally depict the servant's experience as a state that continued for a time in the past. It follows that the awful things that have befallen him have been known to the LORD from the start, and that they belong to a purposeful pattern whose meaning is now being set forth.

The servant has grown up before the LORD *kayyônēq*, "like a green shoot" or, indeed, "like a young child." The green shoot suggests healthy life, and the image implies that the LORD has had his eye on him since childhood. The word occurs as "young child" in a number of texts (e.g., Num. 11:12; Deut. 32:25), not least in the image of the child playing around the viper's den in the paradisal cameo in Isaiah 11:8. LXX takes it as

---

33. LXX alters to "we announced before him" (*anēngeilamen enantion autou*) instead of "he grew up before him." This connects to the "we" speech in v. 1 and makes explicit that the "we" are proclaimers of the message that they have heard.

"child" (*paidion*) in this verse. Curiously, the positive image is immediately followed by "like a root out of arid ground" (*wəkaššōreš mē'ereṣ ṣiyyâ*). "Root" and "shoot" are slightly different images—and arguably come in the wrong order here!— but both convey the idea of new growth. More disturbing in the sequence of the phrases is that a healthy image ("green shoot, child") gives way abruptly to the rather less healthy one of a root emerging from "arid ground" (*ṣiyyâ*), a term that is elsewhere contrasted with well-watered, fertile land (Isa. 35:1; 41:18; cf. Jer. 2:6). How does the poet intend this? Is the root emerging from arid land doomed to wilt and fade, suggesting a life that cannot flourish, and so feeding into the idea of physical unattractiveness that follows (Isa. 53:2b)? Or is this root from arid ground a sign of the new life that will in time make the dry ground lush and fertile (as in 35:1; 41:18)? The poet simply opens both these possible nuances and declines to close down either of them.

In the continuation of the verse (v. 2b), it is the suggestion of unattractiveness and fragility that gains traction, even if the alert reader may justifiably archive the other connotation for use later. The botanical image is laid aside, and the servant is depicted, no longer as seen by the LORD, but set before the gaze of his fellow human beings. The scene is reminiscent of 52:14, in which his appearance was so repugnant that he barely looked human. The line centers on the idea of looking at the beleaguered figure. The verb "to see" is at the heart of it, in the phrase "that we should look at him [*wənir'ēhû*]."[34] And two

34. Our translation takes the phrase "that we should look at him" (*wənir'ēhû*, simple waw plus first-person plural imperfect qal *r'h*, "see") as consequent upon "He had no beauty or noble aspect," i.e., "such that we should look at him." This goes against the MT punctuation, which lets "He had no beauty or noble aspect" stand as a separate clause and groups *wənir'ēhû* with the second half of the line. KJV follows MT, with "and when we shall see him." But our translation is in line with most modern ones.

other terms are formally related to the verb (*tōʾar*, *marʾeh*), translated above as "beauty" and "appearance." Both of these occurred in 52:14b. But now it is the poem's speakers, the "we," who are the subjects of the seeing, those who would in time come to see the servant differently. Yet at this stage he is as if unseen. He had nothing about him to compel attention or admiration; there was no pleasure in looking at him, nothing to attract them to him. The two balancing halves of the line, as set out above, have a certain intensifying progression: there was no reason in his appearance to look at him; still more, there was no reason to *desire* him. The verb *wǝneḥmǝdēhû*, "that we should find him attractive," connotes powerful desire or craving, as in the "coveting" of the tenth commandment (Exod. 20:17).

The line betrays certain unspoken values. Beauty, a noble appearance, natural grace—these are the physical attributes that command attention. They are, indeed, highly regarded in some Old Testament depictions, such as that of the young David (1 Sam. 16:18), or the patriarch Joseph (Gen. 39:6), or the beautiful and virtuous Abigail (1 Sam. 25:3), or Queen Esther (Esther 2:7). All of these possess *tōʾar*, "beauty," as in our text.[35] The word *hādār*, here "noble aspect," can convey an elevated beauty in people or in creation. But it is most frequently applied to the LORD, with the connotation of majesty or splendor (e.g., Isa. 2:10; 35:2), and sometimes in tandem with that most characteristic expression of the LORD's majesty, his "glory" (*kābôd*, Ps. 145:5; cf. Isa. 6:3; Ps. 8:5 [6]).[36]

---

35. The word *tōʾar* is paired with forms of *yāpeh*, "beautiful," in Esther 2:7; 1 Sam. 25:3.

36. The word *hādār* is applied to people in Ps. 45:4 [5] (the king) and Ezek. 16:14 (youthful Israel), and to nature in Isa. 35:2 (Mount Carmel and the plain of Sharon) and Deut. 33:17 (a wild ox). It actually appears twice in Isa. 35:2, of the beauty of both nature and the LORD.

No doubt for this reason, LXX has rendered *ḥādār* here with *doxa*, "glory." As we observed above, LXX lays some emphasis on this concept in relation to the servant. The translator does not want to lose sight of the LORD's declaration in 52:13 that the servant would be exalted, and in this way he carefully maintains the specially close relationship between the servant and the LORD. There is, of course, deep irony in this affirmation of the servant's destined glory and the condition in which he is depicted in chapter 53.

The poem in Hebrew also embeds this irony: the one destined to be exalted must first endure humiliation and pain. But it does not exploit the "glory" nuance of *ḥādār* in the way that LXX does with *doxa*. Its point here is simply to say that the servant had no qualities that marked him out as worthy of admiration according to the ordinary standards by which people judge other people. Like so many people who are virtually invisible in society, he was not worth a second look.

Yet these unspoken values seem to be put in question here. The speakers, as they reflect on their former attitude to the servant, ruefully recall their failure to see the truth. They are not alone in seeing through false pretensions to worth; the sage who penned Proverbs 31, for example, knew the deceitfulness of beauty (Prov. 31:30). But they had gone with the crowd and were blinded by the consensus view.

53:3

nibzeh waḥădal ʾîšîm   ʾîš makʾōbôt wîdûaʿ ḥōlî
He was despised, a man alone,   a man of pain, close companion of sickness.

ûkəmastēr pānîm mimmenû   nibzeh wəlōʾ ḥăšabnuhû

Like one from whom one looks away,   he was despised, and
we considered him to be of no account.

The structure of the verse highlights two things: the double
occurrence of *nibzeh*, "he was despised," loudly declares the
contempt in which the servant was held; and the double occurrence of "man/men" focuses on his raw humanity. The servant's humanity may seem obvious. But the form of verse 3a
is striking. The phrase "a man alone," followed immediately
by "a man . . . ," puts his humanity at the center of the line.
In Hebrew, the words *ʾĭšîm* and *ʾîš*, "men, man," are adjacent,
giving a sharp focus to the line and a correspondence in its parallelism. Moreover, the phrase *waḥădal ʾĭšîm*, "a man alone,"
employs a highly unusual plural form of *ʾîš*, "man," as if to
give extra weight to the structural point.[37]

This man is completely alone. The phrase translated "a man
alone" is more exactly "lacking men." To lack human society
was an affliction in ancient Israel, in which kinship structures
were enormously important and familial obligations powerful.[38]
To be ejected from society put a person in a perilous condition.
Women who lacked a close male relative might be forced into
prostitution (Gen. 38). A prophet whose message became un-
popular could be ostracized and find himself in danger of his
life (Jer. 11:18–23). We are not told why the servant became such
an isolated figure, though we have had a hint of his persecution
in Isaiah 50:4–9. It is implausible to think that he chose it. To

37. The plural form *ʾĭšîm* occurs in only a few places: Ps. 141:4; Prov. 8:4. The
usual form is *ʾănāšîm*.
38. An example that illustrates the difference between Israel's social expectations
and our own is levirate marriage, in which a man had an obligation to raise children
by his deceased brother's widow who would count as the brother's children (Deut.
25:5–10). For an account of the layered kinship structures of family, clan, and tribe in
ancient Israel, see C. J. H. Wright, *God's People in God's Land*, 44–70, and de Vaux,
Ancient Israel, esp. 4–13, 19–23.

be abandoned by friends is one of the worst fates the poets of Israel could imagine (cf. Ps. 88:18 [19]).

There was more to the servant's affliction than loneliness, however; rather, it extended to his physical and psychological life. Nor was his suffering accidental or fleeting; rather, the phrase *ʾîš mak'ōbôt* ("man of pains") implies that he was characterized by pain. The word *mak'ōbôt* can refer to physical pain or to grief or inner turmoil.[39] That his distress was chronic is confirmed by the words that follow, *wîdûaʿ ḥŏlî*, "close companion of sickness." The term *wîdûaʿ* is a part of the verb "to know."[40] The striking image is poignant; here is a man who has no close relationship with people, but he is intimately acquainted with torment.

The servant's isolation is inseparable from the contempt in which he was held. He is "like one from whom one looks away," or, more exactly, "hides one's face." This is explicable not just in terms of revulsion at the ugliness of suffering or deformity, but as a matter of honor and shame. Hiding the face denotes a refusal to have personal interaction. In the Old Testament, it is predominantly the LORD who is said to "hide his face," symbolizing his felt absence from Israel (e.g., Ps. 10:11). Only rarely are humans said to "hide their faces," once when Moses hides his from the LORD, who appears to him in the burning bush (Exod. 3:6),[41] and once when the servant himself *refuses* to "hide his face" from his tormentors (Isa. 50:6). For people to "hide their faces" from the servant is a strong statement that they did not wish to be associated with him in any way, nor even seem to be. He was someone to be avoided at all

39. In its usage, it is not always possible to distinguish between these; cf. Exod. 3:7; Ps. 32:10.
40. It is a qal passive participle masculine singular construct. The construct relationship with *ḥŏlî*, "sickness," creates a strong link between the two terms.
41. This case is akin to the concept that humans cannot look upon the LORD and live (Exod. 33:20; cf. Isa. 6:5).

costs. In this way, his isolation was not just neglect but a willful function of his social context. His rejection from society has become an established and irreversible fact. The phrase "like one from whom one turns away/hides their face" could, by a quirk of Hebrew grammar, also be read as "like one who turns away/hides his face from us."[42] This thought is comprehensible in the context just described, since one so utterly cast out might well become accustomed, or even think it right, to avoid eye contact with anyone they encountered.[43] The precedent of Isaiah 50:6 makes this a less probable interpretation; nevertheless, the poet's predilection for ambiguity prompts the reflection.

The final half-line reiterates the impersonal "he was despised." So far in this verse, the "we" voice has been quiet, while the contempt for the servant has been expressed descriptively. But now in the last phrase it appears again: "we considered him to be of no account," or, put differently, "we did not give him a second thought." The chastened believers thus complete the picture of his suffering by acknowledging that they themselves were complicit in the deep injustice done to him, and they utter, in effect, a confession of guilt.

Afterthought on 53:1–3

These first three verses of chapter 53 conjure up a picture of utter human abjection. In them, the poet continues to shroud the identity of the servant in mystery. The larger interpretive

---

42. The subject of the verb in *ûkəmastēr pānîm* is unspecified ("as one who hides"), and the word *mimmenû*, a suffixed form of the preposition *min*, "from," can mean either "from him" or "from us."

43. This is how Clines understands the phrase we have translated "a man alone" (*ḥădal ʾîšîm*, v. 3), as active, based on an Arabic cognate of *ḥădal*. On this view, the servant is one who holds back, or abstains, from human company (Clines, *I, He, We, and They*, 16).

issues of Isaiah 40–55 retreat temporarily behind this unspar-
ing vision of a human being in pain. As readers, we shelve
the question of whether to imagine him as an individual or
as corporate Israel. We even postpone the concerns that will
very soon occupy us as we read on in chapter 53: How can
such suffering be part of the Lord's purpose, and what has it
to do with salvation? We simply dwell on the terrible fact of
a human being subjected to great torment by the actions and
prejudices of other human beings. The picture connects with
too many life experiences to begin to name, whether they are
our own or those of others. It connects whenever we feel moral
outrage at unjust, inhuman behavior; and it connects when we
become aware that, like the priest and the Levite in the story
of the good Samaritan, we have turned a blind eye to (hidden
our face from) a suffering human being whom we could have
helped.[44] It connects with the passion of Jesus Christ, whose
profound suffering at human hands appalls because it is the
suffering of a human being.

The suffering of one cast out from society is a reflex of
human sin. The point is put memorably by George Herbert
in the second verse of his poem "The Agony," which imagines
the suffering of Christ:

> Who would know Sin, let him repair
> Unto Mount Olivet; there shall he see
> A Man so wrung with pains, that all his hair
> His skin, His garments bloody be.
> Sin is that press and vice, which forceth pain
> To hunt his cruel food through ev'ry vein.[45]

---

44. For the good Samaritan, see Luke 10:29–37 and also Emerson B. Powery's
fine reading of it in the Touchstone Texts series: *The Good Samaritan: Luke 10 for
the Life of the Church*.

45. Herbert, "The Agony," in *The Temple* (1633), quoted in Guite, *Lifting the
Veil*, 34.

■ Isaiah 53:4–6: Wounded because of Our Rebelliousness

53:4

'ākēn ḥŏlāyēnû hû' nāśā'   ûmak'ōbênû səbālām
Surely it was our sicknesses that he bore,   our pains that
he shouldered!

wa'ănaḥnû ḥăšabnuhû nāgûaʿ   mukkēh 'ĕlōhîm ûmə'unneh
Yet we considered him struck down, smitten by God, afflicted!

Here is the turning point in the believers' confession. The
word *'ākēn*, "surely," brings some emotive heft to the strong
affirmations that follow and carries the connotation of a perceived error.[46] With it the perception of the servant pivots into
reverse. The sicknesses and pains, or griefs, that seemed to be
the servant's own are now understood to be "ours"! And far
from somehow deserving them, he was bearing them for "us"!
The reversal is clearly marked by the repetition of the terms
"sicknesses" and "pains" from verse 3. And the structure of
the line brings it out emphatically: "it was *our* sicknesses . . .
our pains" that he bore.

The poet dwells on the servant's "bearing" pain and grief
with the paired verbs in verse 4a (*nāśā'* and *sābal*). At this stage
in the unfolding testimony to the servant, there is no elaboration of what might be entailed in this "bearing." LXX, no
doubt looking ahead to verses 5–6 and 10–12, translates the
first half-line "he bears our sins [*houtos tas hamartias hēmōn
pherei*]." Both Hebrew verbs will recur in verses 11–12 in the
sense of bearing sin. Yet the present line makes no reference

46. The commentator Shalom Paul, citing the medieval Jewish scholar Rashbam,
says it always means "Indeed it is thus, and not as I expected" (Paul, *Isaiah 40–66*,
404). Cf. Gen. 28:16.

to sin, and it simply conveys the sense of being weighed down under a load. Matthew's Gospel finds it to be fulfilled in Jesus's healings of the sick and demon possessed (Matt. 8:17), and in doing so has recognized Jesus's taking on himself the weight of human disease and grief. The trouble of the human condition that the servant bears is not sin alone.

The believers' confession continues in a kind of amazement at their own former incomprehension. The word *wa'ănahnû*, placed at the beginning of verse 4b, has the effect of a strong adversative: "yet we"—a case where the conjunction *wə* is not properly translated by "and." The sense is "We could not have been more wrong!" Their error of judgment confessed in verse 3 is now admitted to be graver. They use the same word as in verse 3, *hăšabnuhû*, "we considered him." But now they confide that their judgment on the servant went beyond mere self-regarding neglect. We might render the phrase expansively as "Yet we actually considered him to be under God's punishment!" This thought in itself should give pause. Even though it comes as part of a confession of error, it is the first hint in the poem that the hand of God might lie directly behind the servant's pain. The idea that human suffering is evidence of God's anger is roundly rejected in both the Old and New Testaments, supremely in the book of Job and also in the teaching of Jesus about a man born blind (John 9). The stance of the poem toward the role of God in the servant's suffering is not straightforward, however; it will return in a more direct statement about the will of God in verse 10 and poses one of the poem's theological challenges. Its awkwardness may already have been felt by the Old Greek translators, who avoided the notion of smiting by God at this point: LXX has merely "but we considered him to be in pain and in affliction and in oppression."[47] That reluctance will

---

47. *Kai hēmeis elogisametha auton einai en ponō kai en plēgē kai en kakōsei.*

be evident again in verse 10. As for the speakers at this point (in the Hebrew text), we cannot tell what exactly they now found wanting in their former attitude. Did they apprehend the false-ness in general of regarding suffering as divine punishment? Perhaps we only have to think that they have realized an error uniquely in relation to the servant. Their confession leaves the question open for now. But it will not go away.

The line in any case accumulates terms for severe punish-ment as a further rhetorical device in this poignant expres-sion of the wrong the speakers had done him. The vocabulary "struck down, smitten, afflicted" belongs to the language of punishment found in other texts.[48] The most striking similari-ties are with Isaiah 1:5–6 and its brutal image of a broken body, perhaps based on the terrible reality of a victim of war. With two forms related to the verb *nkh* (as in "smitten" in our verse) and also *ḥŏlî*, "sickness" (as in our vv. 3–4), the image of the Suffering Servant could even be a reflection on 1:5–6. That broken body symbolized the punishment of Israel for its sin against the Lord; the servant, in contrast, has emphatically not been punished for his own sin. Yet the echo of 1:5–6 raises the question of how the Lord's punishment for sin relates to the broken body of the servant. And the believers show a dawn-ing awareness that it does so, mysteriously, in the relationship between the servant and themselves.

One of the unspoken and unanswered questions posed by the poem concerns what had changed the penitent believers'

48. The form *nāgûaʿ*, here "struck down," is the passive participle of *ngʿ*, "touch," but can mean stricken (by God) with disease (e.g., Job 19:21); *mukkēh*, "smitten," is a hophal participle construct of *nkh*, "strike, smite," often used for punishment by God (e.g., Isa. 1:5; 50:6); *məʿunneh* is a pual participle of *ʿnh*, "afflict." Isa. 1:5 has the form *tukkû*, second-person plural hophal imperfect of *nkh*, echoed in 1:6 by the noun *makkâ*, "[running] sore"; it also has *ḥŏlî*, "sickness." See also 50:6 (of the servant, who gave his back to the "smiters," *ləmakkîm*) and 60:14 (for *məʿannayik*, "those who oppressed you [Israel]").

minds. I think this is of great importance, and we shall return to it in due course.

53:5

wəhû' məḥōlāl mippəšā'ēnû   mədukkā' mē'ăwōnōtênû
Yet he was wounded because of our rebelliousness,   (he was) crushed because of our sinfulness.

mûsar šəlômēnû 'ālāyw   ûbaḥăburātô nirpā'-lānû
On him was the chastisement that made us whole;   and by his scourging, we have been healed.

The believers now meditate further on the relationship between their own sin and the servant's suffering. The structure of these two lines brings out their key thought, an exchange between the servant and "us." This counterpoint between "him" and "us" is maintained in each of the four half-lines that make up the verse. The verse opens by placing the focus firmly on "him": *wəhû'*, "and/yet he." The form does not add to the sense of the phrase that follows: "he was wounded because of our rebelliousness." Rather, its effect is to contradict and negate the false view of him recorded in the preceding line (v. 4b). It helps to express the speakers' complete change of mind about him. Far from being smitten by God, it was on "our" account that he suffered.

The poet conveys the servant's extreme physical abuse in a series of terms in each of the four half-lines. "Wounded" (*məḥōlāl*) implies a stabbing injury (e.g., Ezek. 28:9), sometimes fatal (32:26).[49] It can apply metaphorically to acute distress (Ps. 109:22), but that is not primarily in view here. A little before

---

49. Isa. 53:5 LXX has *etraumatisthē*, "he was wounded."

the present text, in Isaiah 51:9, it is used in a poetic passage about the creation in which the LORD "impales" the mythical primeval Dragon, as also in Job 26:13. The servant is "crushed" (*mədukkāʾ*), a term that can mean "severe oppression" (Isa. 3:15; Ps. 94:5; Prov. 22:22), but like *məḥōlāl*, it too is used of the slaying of a mythical monster (called Rahab in Ps. 89:10 [11]— there in conjunction with *ḥālāl*, "one slain").[50] In the second line of 53:5, the terminology shifts slightly toward an implication of punishment: *mûsar* often has the sense of chastisement for discipline, while *ḥăburātô* denotes bloody wounds of the sort that might come from scourging, perhaps suggesting that the servant has suffered severe judicial corporal punishment.[51] The sequence as a whole does not say unambiguously that the servant died under these terrible abuses, yet they were evidently severe enough to be fatal. Verse 9 will take the depiction further in the direction of the servant's death.

Each of the half-lines has a reference to "us" that corresponds to the description of the servant's pain. In the first two half-lines (v. 5a), the corresponding factor is the speakers' sins. The words *pešaʿ*, "rebellion or rebelliousness," and *ʿāwôn*, "sin or guilt," are found among the extensive vocabulary of sin right at the beginning of Isaiah (1:2–4), the former as a verb (*pāšəʿû*, 1:2b). *Pešaʿ* brings out the aspect of personal revolt against the LORD, depicted in those verses in vivid images of disloyalty and tantamount to a fundamental breach of Israel's covenant with God (cf. Exod. 20:2–3). It resonates with one of the dominant concerns of Isaiah 40–55: that Israel should hold on to faith in the LORD in the face of temptations not to believe in him and to think other gods more powerful. The word *ʿāwôn* is a

---

50. The word *ḥālāl* is a nominal form meaning "one slain," but is evidently related to the verb *ḥālal*, "to be pierced, wounded." The participles *məḥōlāl* (polal) and *mədukkâ* (pual) are passive in meaning.

51. It appears in Isa. 1:6b, of wounds that are "not bound up."

somewhat comprehensive term for the corruption of the human spirit and can embrace sin, guilt, and even punishment. It is telling that the believers put both words in the plural, suggesting that the sins they are confessing were no isolated lapses, but many and habitual.

The terms relating to "us" in the second two half-lines (v. 5b) advance the thought (to salvation). In "the chastisement that made us whole" (*mûsar šəlômēnû*), the term *mûsar* is at home in Proverbs (e.g., 1:2), where it connotes the discipline that leads a young person to wisdom, a sense that is picked up in the LXX translation *paideia* (based on the idea of the education of a child). More than simply "punishment," the term implies endurance that is accepted or imposed for the sake of a good outcome. Here the word is closely joined to *šālôm*: the servant's endurance leads to "our" peace. *Šālôm* is that resonant Old Testament term denoting a fullness of well-being. When translated "peace," it has to be qualified in this way; it is not just an absence of conflict, but corresponds to the deepest human desire for satisfaction. Close to "blessing," it is what anyone might wish or pray for oneself or another. The concept of "wholeness" has no limits, but is open to searching exploration. It might apply to an individual in terms of physical and psychological well-being, and embraces everything that can be understood about the health of the human psyche. Equally, it might apply to a community, small or large, in terms of its inner relations, characterized by truth and security and whatever makes for the good of all.

The phrase *mûsar šəlômēnû 'ālāyw* is tantalizingly laconic and almost impossible to translate in a way that captures its effect; "the chastisement of our wholeness [was upon him]" merely invites some further comment on its meaning. Our translation, "the chastisement that made us whole," is an attempt to tease out the meaning, expressing the relationship of the words *mûsar šəlômēnû* in terms of consequence. But the effect of the phrase is to affirm the tightest possible relationship between the concepts. In this way it articulates, with the greatest irony and pathos, the stark contrast between the suffering of the servant and the desired outcome for "us."

The final phrase in verse 5, *ûbaḥăburātô nirpāʾ lānû*, enhances the thought with greater syntactical transparency: "by his scourging, we have been healed." The undefined "punishment" (in *mûsar*) is now specified as a brutal wounding, and the benefit to "us" is our "healing." Healing is a common metaphor for salvation and restoration, notably in Isaiah 6:10.[52] Its pairing here with the image of bloody wounds is fitting. But once again the effect is poignant: the healing that follows this scourging is not given to the one who is wounded, but to "us," who have not been subjected to it.

While verse 5 establishes a close link between the servant's suffering and the benefits that come to the "we" speakers as a result, the poem does not yet explain the way in which this exchange was accomplished. The relationship between the suffering and the benefits is expressed in both parts of verse 5a by the simple preposition *min*, "from," translated here as "because of."[53] Much can hang on a preposition! Standard translations, no doubt under the powerful influence of the KJV, predominantly render this "from" as "for." This tends toward the sense that the suffering had the purpose of making atonement for sins. To put it differently, it implies that the servant suffered vicariously, accepting in "our" stead a penalty that was due to

---

52. See also Isa. 19:22; 57:18–19; Jer. 3:22; 17:14; 30:12–13; 33:6; Hosea 6:1; 7:1; 11:3; 14:4 [5].

53. In the form *mēʿăwōnōtênû*, "because of our sins," *min* alters in form to *mē* because it precedes the guttural consonant ʿ, a regular morphological change in biblical Hebrew.

"us" because of our sins. When taken together with verses 6, 8, and 10–11, this interpretation of verse 5 becomes unavoidable. It is understood accordingly in New Testament texts such as 1 Peter 2:22–25 and Romans 4:24–25. We will say more about these texts in the following chapter.

The argument for a vicarious understanding of Isaiah 53:5 is best made by reference to the text's context and reception, rather than by making too much of prepositions.[54] For this reason the neutral "because of" is preferred in our translation (with NJPS). The speakers do not tell us why they thought the servant's suffering was because of their sins. People sometimes feel guilty because someone has suffered unjustly, and they think perhaps it should have been them instead of the victim. "Survivor guilt" is a case of it. This could be a sufficient explanation of what the believers speaking as "we" are saying at this stage. However, they have not yet finished with their reflection on the meaning of the servant's suffering, as will emerge as the poem continues.

53:6

kullānû kaṣṣō'n tā'înû   'îš lədarkô pānînû
All of us, like sheep, have gone astray;   each one has turned
  on to his own path;

wyhwh hipgîa' bô   'ēt 'ăwōn kullānû.
yet the LORD brought on him   the sinfulness of us all.

In verse 6, the nature of the exchange between the servant's innocent suffering and "our" sin and benefit begins to be spelled out. The speakers now make a direct confession of sin. Their

---

54. LXX has the preposition *dia*, "through, because of," which can have a range of meanings according to context. It is consistent with a vicarious reading but does not compel it.

speech as "we" is accentuated by the double use of the term
kullānû ("we all, all of us"), which both opens and closes the
verse. What is the reach of this "all"? In 50:9, the word *kullām*,
"all of them," denotes the servant's enemies, whose opposition
to him would infallibly fail. In the present case, the "we all"
might apply to the undefined group that now speaks; or the
echo of 50:9 could imply that they identify themselves, in confessional mode, with those who had been the servant's enemies.
Most likely, the confessing group is referring to all Israel, as
suggested by 51:18, where the poet laments that there was none
among "all the sons" of Jerusalem who could guide her truly.
The accent on totality is further enhanced by the individual-
izing "each one has turned on to his own path" in the second
half of 53:6a.[55] It is a sweeping confession of sin, which need
not be confined to the specific moral failures that caused the
servant's agonies, but reaches back through generations and
thus corresponds to the prophet's perspective on the whole
history of Israel, as in 1:2–4.[56]

In the common biblical metaphor, sheep are in constant need
of guidance by a shepherd (Ps. 23), and the danger of going
astray, or turning into a self-chosen path, is a serious threat to
life. This underlies Jesus's view of the crowds he ministered
to, in that they were "like sheep without a shepherd" (Matt.
9:36), his reply to a Canaanite woman that he was sent only to
the "lost sheep of the house of Israel" (15:24), and his parable
about the farmer who went in search of one lost sheep among
his flock of a hundred (18:10–14). The idea of people as sheep
and their rulers as shepherds is rooted in the imagination of
a rural, pastoral economy and lends itself to development in
various ways (e.g., Ezek. 34; Zech. 11). In the picture of sheep

55. "Each one" translates the noun *'îš*, "a man," used idiomatically here in this
distributive sense.
56. Other texts may be cited, such as 57:1–13.

going astray, the dominant notion is danger; the wandering sheep are vulnerable to pitfalls in a rocky terrain and to predators. This thought also underlies Jesus's image of himself as the "good shepherd" (John 10:1–6).

When people are described as going astray like sheep, the idea shades over readily into sin. The verb used in Isaiah 53:6a (*tāʿînû*) often has this sense; it is wandering from the safe path of the Shepherd, the LORD, who knows what their security and well-being requires.[57] The path that is "right" for sheep is also a path of "righteousness," in the neat ambiguity of "right paths/paths of righteousness" in Psalm 23:3 (*bəmaʿgəlê ṣedeq*). In Isaiah 28:7, "wandering" implies a fatal loss of vision and understanding. The speakers' confession in 53:6a, therefore, is an admission both of sin and of the folly of having allowed themselves to fall into great danger.

The connection between "our" sin and the servant's suffering being developed in verses 4–6 takes a new turn in verse 6b, when it is said for the first time that his affliction has been caused by the LORD. The point is accentuated by the placement of *wyhwh* ("yet the LORD") in first position in the line. The word "yet" translates the conjunction *w-* prefixed to *yhwh*, which is more commonly "and." But it often bears the adversative sense of "but" or "yet," where a contrast is implied with something in the preceding text, especially when it is joined with a noun in the emphatic first position in a line. Verse 6b conveys the unexpected fact (rhetorically speaking) that the effects of "our" sinfulness have been laid by the LORD, not on "us," but on "him." The counterpoint of "him" and "us" is expressed powerfully by the parallel positions in the line of *bô* ("on him") and *kullānû* ("us all"), each element falling at the end of its half-line. The

---

57. Texts that use the verb *tāʿâ*, "wander," in this sense include Isa. 28:7; 29:4; 35:8; 47:15; Ezek. 14:11; Pss. 58:3 [4]; 119:176.

line as a whole is an elaboration of the exchange between "us" and the servant, with the new twist that this has been a deliberate act of the LORD. The point is especially striking, because in verse 4 the speakers confessed their mistaken view that he had been "smitten" and "afflicted" by God. The difference in what they say here is that, whereas they had previously thought that his suffering must be due to his own sin, they now realize that it was due to theirs.

The statement is extraordinary. In verse 5, the servant's suffering was admittedly closely linked to "our" sin: he was "crushed because of our sinfulness [mē'ăwōnōtênû]." This might have been understood as an unintended consequence of the speakers' sinfulness. But that explanation is not possible for verse 6b. The "sinfulness" is denoted by the same noun as in verse 5; 'ăwōn kullānû, "the sinfulness of us all," is virtually the same as 'ăwōnōtênû, "our sinfulness," in that verse. But here, the intentional connection between the speakers' sin and the servant's suffering, in the mind of the LORD, is inescapable. It is the LORD who has "brought [it] on him" (hipgîa' bô), a causative hiphil form expressing agency. The same LORD who spoke in the first line of the poem, drawing attention to "my servant" and his exaltation (52:13), is here the author of his wretchedness.[58]

How can we make sense of this? Is it an instance of the Old Testament's tendency to attribute everything that happens to God, as a kind of logical corollary of its confession of him as the only God? It is the LORD who casts down and raises up, who brings disaster as well as good (Hosea 6:1–2), the God who both brought the great flood of Genesis and saved

58. LXX renders the line "the LORD gave him over to our sins" (*kurios paredōken auton tais hamartiais hēmōn*). LXX tends to diminish the idea of the servant's atoning death, both here and in v. 10. As regards the LORD's agency in his suffering, it seems to be taken in a permissive sense (the LORD allowed the servant to suffer the consequences of our sins), while avoiding the idea of vicarious suffering.

a renewed humanity from the wreckage (Gen. 6:5–9:17). This insight provides a partial explanation, but the line invites us to look deeper. At the heart of it is the deliberateness of the exchange: God brought on *him* the sinfulness of *us all*. This is no mere corollary of monotheism; rather, it expresses the mystery of the transcendent God's involvement in the affairs of the world, a place where his sovereign freedom meets the limited but untrammeled freedoms of human action. This is the theological premise that undergirds the book of Isaiah. Kingdoms rise and fall in accord with their own lights and decisions, in lines of causation that are open to the historian to describe; and at the same time, the LORD pursues his "plans" in sovereign engagement with them, but in ways that elude the historian's grasp.[59] This is what Katherine Sonderegger calls "compatibilism."[60] It is not simply a case of dual description, in which one can see a reality differently from different angles, but a way of conceptualizing the mysterious idea of God acting in and through ordinary events. In the present case, it has in it the seed of catastrophic conflict. If one were to take the trajectory of the servant out of the book of Isaiah, one would be left with a purging of Israel through their deep humiliation and a kind of victory of Israel's God over other gods and their client kings. But this would be a story doomed to endless repetition and an unsatisfactory resolution of the deepest problems of the human condition. The irreconcilable conflict between the sovereign freedom of God and the real freedoms of human beings is brought to a head in the LORD bringing on *him* the sinfulness of *us all*. It bears repeating that the word ʿāwôn, here translated "sinfulness," suggests the complex interplay between

---

59. For the motif of the LORD's plans in critical dialogue with the nations' plans, see Isa. 5:19; 7:5–9; 8:10; 14:14–27; 19:3, 11–12, 17; 25:1; 28:29; 30:1; 36:5; 44:26; 46:10–11.

60. Sonderegger, *Systematic Theology*.

sin, guilt, and punishment. The intention of the LORD's action through the servant is nothing less than a deliverance from this self-induced nexus of moral enslavement and the renewing of the human condition. In the servant's suffering, there is a presence of both God and humanity in the unmaking and remaking of the human. The servant's active participation in this drama is neatly captured in the final phrase of verse 12, "[he] makes intercession for the rebels," where the verb "makes intercession" is *yapgîaʿ*, the same verb as in "the LORD *brought on* him" in verse 6. This echo secures a tight relationship in the poem between the LORD's action and that of the servant.

Afterthought on 53:4–6

These verses depend, as we saw, on a conversion. But what brought it about? The confessing group do not tell us, and we have no access to a "historical" answer to the question. Perhaps it is best considered as a "spiritual" one. The poet Malcolm Guite points us to the case of Nathanael in John 1:43–51, in a way that I think illuminates our text. Nathanael makes an unpromising start when he hears the call of Jesus through Philip and replies, "Can anything good come out of Nazareth?" (1:46 NRSV). Jesus anticipates him, however. Seeing him a little way off, Jesus says, "Here is truly an Israelite in whom there is no deceit!" (1:47 NRSV). Nathanael is amazed by the fact that Jesus already knows him and had seen him sitting under a fig tree (a delightful detail!), and he immediately confesses faith: "Rabbi, you are the Son of God! You are the King of Israel!" (1:49 NRSV). Guite notes the motif of "seeing" in this encounter.[61] Philip says, "Come and see" (v. 46). Jesus sees Nathanael coming toward him (v. 47). Jesus says of Nathanael's new belief,

---

61. Guite, *Lifting the Veil*, 23.

"You will see greater things than these," and again, "You will see heaven opened and the angels of God ascending and descending upon the Son of Man" (vv. 50–51 NRSV). The allusion to the patriarch Jacob's vision of a ladder up to heaven is unmistakable (Gen. 28:10–17), but now Jesus himself, the Son of Man, is the ladder. Guite says of Nathanael's dramatic change of mind, "This is an example in the Gospel of a sudden 'awakening,' a direct pointing to reality, which some people think is only associated with Buddhism, but here it is in the Gospel!"[62]

The motif of "seeing," as comprehension of the deepest truths about God, also runs through Isaiah. The converted group of speakers, unlike the people of Israel in the prophet Isaiah's day (Isa. 6:9–10; 29:9–14), have come to "see." In doing so, they fulfill the prophecy of a future time: "Out of their gloom and darkness the eyes of the blind shall see" (Isa. 29:18 NRSV). What they have come to see is so unexpected and extraordinary that it is easy to understand why they were slow to accept it. Everything is counterintuitive. The idea that one should pay the penalty for the sins of another was alien to the thought of Old Testament people. It is the basic assumption of Old Testament thought and rhetoric that all who are addressed are capable and duty-bound to repent and change, and that people should pay the penalty for their own sin. The prophet Ezekiel devotes a chapter to the point (Ezek. 18), and a law in Deuteronomy gives another angle on it (Deut. 24:16). One might find a counterindication in Exodus 20:5–6, but this is capable of other interpretations.[63] Likewise the books of Kings, with their sense of guilt accruing over generations (e.g., 2 Kings 23:26–27), never override the premise

62. Guite, *Lifting the Veil*, 25.
63. It can, I think, be understood to refer to the dire effects of sin percolating down through time.

of individual or generational accountability, as is clear from the prophetic summation in 2 Kings 17:13–18. The story of judgment in Kings is not one of people suffering for the sin of others, but rather of God's sovereign decision no longer to tolerate persistent sin.

Isaiah 53 breaks this mold in an extraordinary way. It does so, not by simply contradicting the Old Testament theological heritage, but by introducing something completely new, whose meaning lies in the mystery of God's incarnation. The topic returns in subsequent verses of Isaiah 53 and will arise when we finally try to make sense of the chapter as a whole in terms of the life, death, and resurrection of Christ.[64]

▓ Isaiah 53:7–9: He Said Not a Word

These verses elaborate on the nature of the servant's suffering, hinting at his death. Yet they are reticent about disclosing details; rather, they emphasize his innocence and quiet submission.

53:7

niggaś wəhûʾ naʿăneh   wəlōʾ yiptaḥ-pîw

He was sore pressed, though already bowed down;   yet he said not a word.

kaśśeh laṭṭebaḥ yûbāl   ûkərāḥēl lipnê gōzəzeyhā neʾĕlāmâ

Like a lamb brought to the slaughter,   or as a ewe before her shearers is silent,

---

64. Some modern thinkers too have balked at the idea of suffering for the sins of others. The German philosopher Immanuel Kant believed as a matter of principle that personal responsibility for guilt was inalienable. Yet there is a theological tradition that explores the possible connotations of vicarious sin-bearing, making a notable distinction between "representation" and "substitution." See Janowski, "He Bore Our Sins," 51–54, and below, chap. 4.

wəlō' yiptaḥ pîw

he said not a word.

The speaking voice in verses 7–9 is no longer overtly the "we" who have spoken in verses 1–6. In verse 8, an "I" voice is heard in "my people." This could be the LORD or the prophet (as in Jer. 8:22). More likely it is a melding of the voices of the LORD, the prophet, and the "we" group, who have come to understand the truth about the servant. The confession of the "we" has been subsumed into the dominant, authoritative voice of the poem.[65]

The servant's suffering is conveyed in progressive images. It is expressed, first, as severe oppression and affliction. The word for "sore pressed" is in a niphal form that occurs in only two other Old Testament texts: in 1 Samuel 13:6, it refers to the army of Israel under unbearable pressure from Philistine forces; and in Isaiah 3:5, it depicts social breakdown in Israel, in which each person becomes an oppressor to everyone else.[66] The word translated "bowed down" (*na'ăneh*), also a niphal form, can mean "to humble oneself" (as in Exod. 10:3) or "to be humbled or afflicted" (Isa. 58:10).[67] As a participle following the indicative form *niggaś*, it takes on a circumstantial sense, "he being bowed down," or, as more loosely translated here, "though already bowed down." The effect is to suggest relentless brutality: kicking a man when he is down.

The picture is elaborated by the motif of the servant's silence. In spite of his abuse, "he said not a word," or, more

---

65. Clines also speaks, slightly differently, of a merging of perspectives in the poem, showing how "he" stands in a similar relationship to both the "we" and the "they" (*I, He, We, and They*, 40).

66. The form is the niphal of *nāgaś*, a verb whose qal form means "to drive or press."

67. The form *na'ăneh* is the niphal participle of *'ānâ* II.

exactly, "he did not open his mouth." His unprotesting submission to violence is emphasized by the double occurrence of the phrase in the verse. It is elaborated by two images drawn from shepherding. There is an ironic shift from the use of a sheep metaphor to denote the confessing sinners' proneness to stray in verse 6, to its application in a different way to the servant in verse 7; now sheep typify uncomplaining acquiescence while things are done to them. In the first image, the lamb is led to the slaughter, while in the second the mature ewe submits to its shearers. Here the sheep is not merely silent but dumb (*ne'ĕlāmâ*), as if unable to speak. The images were no doubt vivid to a herding society. They are employed here to denote the servant's acquiescence in what was happening to him.

While the images enhance the motif of silence, their content is not accidental. Lambs and sheep are vulnerable, subject to the will of both shepherds and predators. The lamb led to the slaughter is ominous for the servant; even the less drastic shearing image has a hint of forceful subjection.[68]

The servant's quiet acquiescence is a vital element in his portrayal. It is not accidental that when the apostle Philip encounters the Ethiopian official reading Isaiah 53, it is verses 7–8 that he is focusing on and that prompt his question about who the text refers to (Acts 8:32–33). As we have noticed concerning verse 5 above, the same image is picked up in 1 Peter 2:23. The willingness of Jesus to accept his own terrible fate evidently made a powerful impact on his first followers; and this is reflected in the New Testament writers' appropriation of Isaiah 53:7.

---

68. There is perhaps a creative sound-echo between *gōzazeyhā*, "her shearers," and *niggaś*, "he was sore pressed." I think there is a similar echo between the verbs *gzz* and *ngś* in Deut. 15, in *lō'-yiggōś* (15:2) and *wəlō' tāgōz* (15:19).

53:8

mē'ōṣer ûmimmišpāṭ luqqaḥ   wə'et-dôrô mî yəśôḥēaḥ

By a corruption of justice he was taken off,   and as for his generation, who gave thought

kî nigzar mē'ereṣ ḥayyîm   mippeša' 'ammî nega' lāmô

to the fact that he had been cut off from the land of the living?   Because of the sin of my people, the blow fell on him.

Here we get tantalizingly close to "what really happened" to the servant. He is said to have been "taken off" and "cut off from the land of the living," two passive verb forms that once again highlight his victimhood. It emerges more clearly here than before that definite actions were taken against him, though it remains unclear what exactly they were. The first phrase has judicial connotations. The word *'ōṣer* occurs only a few times in the Old Testament, denoting some kind of constraint or holding in.[69] Combined with *mišpāṭ*, "justice, judgment," it suggests a stage in a legal process, such as arrest or imprisonment, hence John Goldingay's translation of the phrase, "by legal restraint."[70] "He was taken off" (*luqqaḥ*) would then mean that he was carried off to jail. One well-known reading of Isaiah 53 builds its interpretation of the servant's fate on this premise.[71] In my view, this goes further than the text allows, and falls into the trap of subjecting it to a speculative historical

---

69. In Ps. 107:39 it apparently means "oppression." In Prov. 30:16 it refers to a closed womb, albeit in a disputed text. The verb *'āṣar*, formally related to *'ōṣer*, means "retain, hold back," and is used by Jeremiah to mean that he is prevented by the royal authorities from going to the temple (Jer. 36:5), possibly because he is in prison (33:1; 39:15).

70. Goldingay, *Message of Isaiah 40–55*, 506.

71. Whybray, *Thanksgiving for a Liberated Prophet*.

reconstruction that is then used to resolve its obscurities. The translation offered here ("by a corruption of justice") picks up the connotation of oppression in ʿōṣer and understands the text to mean that there was something abusive or coercive about the measures taken against him.

The verb "taken off," or simply "taken,"[72] could mean several things, including "captured," "killed,"[73] or, conceivably, "rescued."[74] Our best guide on this is the parallel line, "he had been cut off from the land of the living." So it can hardly be understood in a positive sense. In the flow of the poem, it could imply that the servant was removed from public view. This can be well understood as a reaction of authorities to one who was having a disturbing effect on the populace. He is depicted in verses 2–3 as one from whom people instinctively recoiled. In his isolation he has been physically abused, whether by authorities or by others for their own vindictive reasons. It might seem wise to remove him from the scene on a trumped-up charge for the sake of maintaining good public order. The royal officials in Jeremiah's time certainly thought like this (Jer. 38:4), as did Pontius Pilate, when the anger of Jesus's enemies caused Pilate to fear a riot (Matt. 27:24).

The verse moves from the assertion that the servant was "cut off" to a further assertion that this was for the sin of others. It begins to do this by drawing "his generation" (dôrô) into the picture. The servant has been implicitly surrounded by others throughout his portrayal: kings; people who despised him; the "we" speakers in verses 1–6; people who have actively persecuted him and deprived him of justice. How "his generation"

---

72. The form luqqaḥ is third masculine singular perfect pual of lāqaḥ, "take."

73. See Ezek. 33:4, where the sword "takes" the person who does not respond to prophetic warning; cf. Prov. 24:11 (though there the fate of death is explicit).

74. "Rescued" is plausible because of the preposition min, "from," in both elements of the expression mēʿōṣer ûmimmišpāṭ: i.e., "he was taken away from oppression and justice"; the translation above treats the phrase as in effect a hendiadys.

fits into the picture is not immediately obvious, partly because the phrase is not easy to interpret. Our translation follows one of the common interpretations of the words *wə'et-dôrô mî yəśôḥēaḥ*: "as for his generation, who gave thought [to the fact . . .]?" This takes the particle *'et* in *wə'et-dôrô* as a preposition meaning "in respect of," and in effect makes "his generation" the subject of the verb *yəśôḥēaḥ*, "ponder" or "consider."[75] The phrase thus has to be run on to the next line: "who gave thought to the fact that . . . ?" This reading (like so much else in the poem) is not certain for several reasons. First, it is awkward, out of keeping with the dominant style of the poem, which mostly falls into self-contained half-lines, creating regular rhythms and balances. Second, the little word *'et* functions much more commonly as a semantic signal (untranslatable in itself) that the word immediately following is a definite direct object.[76] The phrase could, therefore, be read as a self-contained half-line, where "his generation" is the object of the verb *yəśôḥēaḥ*. This entails finding an alternative meaning for the key word *dôrô* (since "Who considered his generation?" makes little sense). Other possibilities include "Who considered his dwelling place?" and "Who considered his state?" (or perhaps "fate").[77]

In this case as in others, the text resists certainty in its interpretation. The notion that it was the servant's "generation" that had failed to understand him is a different angle from that of

75. The form *yəśôḥēaḥ* is a polel of the verb *śiaḥ*, "muse," and means "meditate, consider"; cf. Ps. 143:5.

76. A "definite" noun is one such as "the horse" or "his horse" or a proper name; that is, where a particular one of the kind is in view, rather than, e.g., "a horse."

77. In Isa. 38:12, the word *dôr* means "dwelling," and this spatial sense is adopted here by NJPS. But it is not used elsewhere in this sense in the Hebrew Bible and is not an obvious improvement here. "State" or "fate" is based on meanings in Akkadian and Arabic, Semitic languages that often have vocabulary overlaps with Hebrew (see Clines, *I, He, We, and They*, 18; Paul, *Isaiah 40–66*, 408). The word *dôr* may bear a meaning like this in Ps. 24:6.

verses 1–6, where it was the "we" speakers who confessed their incomprehension. Yet there is a certain resonance between that account of a former failure and this new idea in verse 8. At the height of his suffering, no one even gave a second thought to the cause or meaning of it.

The servant was not only "taken off" but was "cut off from the land of the living." The expression can imply that he was killed, as in the very similar saying in Jeremiah 11:19; there Jeremiah complained that he was led, unsuspectingly, "like a lamb to the slaughter" and that his enemies wished to kill him and blot out his name from memory.[78] In some texts, however, the verb *gāzar*, "cut/cut off," does not mean death, but some other disastrous disruption of life (e.g., Ezek. 37:11; Lam. 3:54). Conceivably, the poet is using a forceful expression to depict the servant's extreme rejection. In any case, the effect of the line is to show the gaping chasm between the thoughtless view of him by his contemporaries and the reality of what was happening to him. The picture calls to mind Jesus's prayer for his tormentors on the cross, "Father, forgive them; for they do not know what they are doing" (Luke 23:34 NRSV).

If the servant's fate in verse 8b is not as clear as we would like it to be, Luke in Acts had little doubt about it. The LXX form of Isaiah 53:8, which Philip and the Ethiopian official had before them, reads:

> In his humiliation judgment was taken from him.
> Who can describe his generation?
> For his life is taken up from the earth.

LXX has slightly smoothed the first line, and for the second has taken one of the options outlined above. As for the final

---

78. The verb for "cut off" in Jer. 11:19 is *kārat*, whereas in Isa. 53:8 it is *gāzar*; but there is no observable difference between them in these verses.

line, LXX itself may simply be following the Hebrew. Yet it is clear that Luke and Philip have understood the verse to speak of Jesus's still-recent death and resurrection. A text that for them might have been obscure has leapt into life because they have come to know the risen Christ.

The final half-line of 53:8 is a further ironic expression of the relationship between the servant's suffering and the sin of others. The counterpoint of "the sin of my people" and "the blow [that] fell on him" recalls the similar interplay between "him" and "us" in verse 5. The line itself is compact, however, and in its details can be read in a number of ways. First, it is somewhat surprising to find the designation "my people," because the ones for whom the servant suffered have not previously been named in this way in the poem, and the form of verses 7–8 to this point leads us to expect another reference to "him/his." The Great Isaiah Scroll from Qumran (1QIsaᵃ) actually has the reading ʿammô, "his people," instead of MT's ʿammî, "my people." It is a small difference in the Hebrew script and could easily be due to a moment of inattention on the Qumran scribe's part, yet it is readily explained by his expectation of consistency with the immediately preceding lines. For the same reason, it is harder to imagine a slip from an original "his people" to the surprising "my people" by a Masoretic scribe, so "my people" is likelier to be original.[79] The unexpectedness of the form is an effect created by the poem to bring the voice of the LORD into focus. Since verse 7, the poem has tended to meld the voices of the "we" speakers, the poet, and the LORD. The first-person singular in "my people" could be the LORD or the poet, or, better, the poet expressing the view of the LORD. It is the first time since 52:13 that the LORD has spoken directly; but we are now reminded

---

79. LXX also has "my people," *tou laou mou*.

that he has been closely present behind the servant's portrayal all along.

The people's "sin" is *pešaʿ*, one of the terms that appeared in verse 5, here used resumptively. The "blow" that has fallen (*negaʿ*) recalls verse 4, where the verbal form, *nāgûaʿ*, "stricken," was part of the description of the servant's suffering. The "blow" stands for all that was hinted at there. But what exactly is being said about it? A glance at standard translations shows a divergence: Does it mean that the blow fell *on him* (NIV, ESV, NRSV) or that it *should have* fallen on those "to whom the stroke was due" (JPS, NASB)? This puzzle arises from the teasing ambiguity of the laconic Hebrew phrase *negaʿ lāmô*, because the word *lāmô* is a poetic form that, oddly, can mean either "to him" or "to them." The poet could have made it plainer by using a more regular form.[80] The ambiguity results not only from the choice of the prepositional form, however, but from the absence of syntax in the phrase. Nothing in the Hebrew corresponds to "that fell" or "that should have fallen." Once again, the poet has chosen to make the reader fill the gaps, and in this way to reflect on the possibilities created by the language.[81] The different decisions made by the standard translations, as noted above, are part of this interpretive activity.

80. The word *lāmô* is a compound form based on the preposition *lǝ*, "to, for." The regular forms *lô* ("to him") and *lāhem*, or *lām* ("to them"), are also compounded with *lǝ*.

81. The ancient versions show further evidence of puzzlement over the text. 1QIsaᵃ has the verb *nwgaʿ* (apparently the pual *nuggaʿ*, meaning "he was struck") instead of the noun *negaʿ*, giving a more transparent syntax. LXX has the significantly different *ēchthē eis thanaton*, "he was led to death." This apparently reads the Hebrew verb *nāgâ*, "lead," instead of the similar-looking *nāgaʿ*, "strike," as found in MT and 1QIsaᵃ. The addition of "to death" could be based on a Hebrew text that had *lammāwet* rather than *lāmô*, which would require only a slight difference in the consonantal text (the addition of a *tav*: *lmw*/*lmwt*). LXX may have had a corrupt Hebrew text or was simply puzzled by what it saw. Its rendering "to death" was probably influenced by its interpretation of the poem as a whole.

53:9

wayyittēn 'et-rəšā'îm qibrô   wə'et-'āšîr bəmōtāyw
They made his grave with the wicked   and his tomb with
  the rich,

'al lō'-ḥāmās 'āśâ   wəlō' mirmâ bəpîw
yet he did no violence   or uttered a word of deceit.

Like the preceding verse, this one begins by taking the narrative a little further and ends with an evaluative comment. Having "taken him off," the servant's enemies have now "made his
grave."[82] The expression is most naturally taken to mean that the
servant actually died and was buried. The reference to his death
is oblique, however, since the chief impact of the half-line is
that his grave was made "with the wicked," presumably in some
place of dishonor. This pursues the thought in the poem that
the servant was treated unjustly; it was an injustice that this final
disgrace should be heaped upon him, that in his death he should
be considered a miscreant, when in fact he was innocent. "The
wicked" might be generic, or a particular group that in the poet's
view merited the name, perhaps those who refused to heed the
prophetic command to flee Babylon (Isa. 48:20–22); they are in
any case not identified. More important is the stress on disgrace
and injustice. This point would actually stand even if the servant
did not die; it is sometimes held that the line could mean merely
that a disgraceful burial was planned for the servant.[83]

---

82. The verb *wayyitēn* is singular: "and he/one gave/made," but the subject is not
specified, and the sense is impersonal, as in the English impersonal "they." 1QIsa^a
has the plural *wytnû*.
    83. Clines points to a text in the ancient Babylonian wisdom poem *Ludlul bēl nēmeqi*
(II:114–15) in which the poet laments that funeral arrangements and a grave have been
prepared for him while he is still in life (Clines, *I, He, We, and They*, 28). Shalom Paul also
makes the point (*Isaiah 40–66*, 408). Both cite Lambert, *Babylonian Wisdom Literature*, 46.

The second half-line of verse 9a closely parallels the first: "his grave" is echoed by "his tomb," and "the wicked" corresponds to "the rich." Both elements tell us something of the poet's art. Just as the servant's grave was "with the wicked," so his tomb is "with the rich" or perhaps "with a rich man." The curious parallelism between "wicked" and "rich" has raised some eyebrows and led to suggested emendations.[84] However, we should not be surprised by this text's bold inventiveness. The poet has created a sound-echo between *ʿāšîr*, "rich," and *rəšāʿîm*, "wicked," and so has used the technique of poetic parallelism to produce an arresting effect.[85] The thought has analogies in the prophetic literature, where wealth sometimes has the connotation of ill-gotten gain. The best example is Micah 6:10–13, which has a parallel between "wicked" and "rich" resembling the one in our text.[86]

As for "his tomb," this is a rendering of the anomalous Hebrew *bəmōtāyw*. It is anomalous because it looks like a plural form of the word *māwet*, "death," prefixed by the preposition *bə*, hence "in his deaths." *Māwet* appears nowhere else in the

---

84. For example, Paul notes the proposed emendation of *ʿāšîr* to *ʿōśê raʿ*, "doers of evil," among other suggestions (Paul, *Isaiah 40–66*, 409). But there is no textual evidence for such a change, and it merely substitutes a bland text for an interesting one!

85. The sound-echo is even closer in 1QIsaᵃ, which apparently has the plural *ʿāšîrîm*, "rich men" (though the text is hard to read). LXX also has the plural, *tous plousious*, albeit in a somewhat divergent text.

86. Note the verbal play on *rāšāʿ*, *rešaʿ*, "wicked, wickedness" (vv. 10–11), and *ʿăšîreyhā*, "[whose] rich men" (v. 12). Goldingay notes other similarities between the Micah passage and Isa. 53:9 (*Message of Isaiah 40–55*, 509). See also Jer. 17:11. Readers of the Gospels will be aware of a resonance of Isa. 53:9 in the record of Joseph of Arimathea taking the body of the crucified Jesus for burial in his tomb. All four Gospels have an account of this, but it is interesting that only Matthew notes that he was "a rich man" (Matt. 27:57; see also Mark 15:42–47; Luke 23:50–56; John 19:38–42). Luke notes only that Joseph was "good and righteous" and was "waiting expectantly for the kingdom of God" (23:50–51 NRSV). Matthew may have had an eye on Joseph's action as a possible fulfillment of prophecy; but the other Gospel writers may have been alert to the fact that "rich" is paralleled by "wicked" in Isa. 53:9 and therefore avoided noting Joseph's wealth.

plural and is in any case rather odd. If the poet meant "in his death," why did he not use the expected singular form *bəmôtô*? Because of this oddity, and with some support from the Great Isaiah Scroll, *bəmōtāyw* is widely read as a form of the word *bāmâ*, even though in this case too it is not a correct form.[87] The word *bāmâ* usually refers to a place of worship, or what the book of Kings (e.g., 1 Kings 3:2–3) calls "high places,"[88] and it may be attested in the meaning "memorial stele," or "grave marker" (Ezek. 43:7).[89]

It is a mark of the poet's art that, in his choice of words, he has let us play with the variants "tomb" and "death"; *bəmōtāyw* is not explicitly either, yet we entertain both possibilities. Standard translations—which must make decisions where readers of poetry do not—diverge on the point, showing a slight preponderance of "in his death." The inevitable hesitation is manifest in NRSV's revision of RSV's "in his death" to "his tomb." In reading the line, we find ourselves compelled to reflect on the likely meaning in the context of the poem as a whole. The essential point of the line is, however, that the servant is consigned not only to death but to the terrible fate of a dishonorable memory in Israel.

The verse returns, in its second line, to the motif of the servant's innocence and undeserved suffering. The stark discrepancy between his savage treatment and his innocence is evident in the simple juxtaposition of the two lines. The causal relationship between them is somewhat muted because of the unusual use of the word *'al* at the beginning of the second line;

---

87. The expected form would be *bāmōtāyw* (cf. Num. 33:52, *bāmōtām*).

88. 1QIsa[a] has the form *bwmtw* (= *bômātô*).

89. The form in Ezek. 43:7 is *bāmôtām*, "their high places"; the context suggests that these "high places" serve as the kings' burial monuments. LXX sometimes translates *bāmâ* with *stēlē*, "monument, pillar" (e.g., Lev. 26:30). Some modern translations of Ezek. 43:7, however, understand the form to be based on *māwet*, "death," reading *bəmôtam*, "in their death" (NRSV, NASB).

normally a preposition meaning "on" or "against," it stands here for the conjunction ʿal ʾăšer. This might be understood as "although," but could also be a heavily ironic "because"—he was persecuted precisely because of his innocence.[90] The temporal relationship between his persecution and his innocence is not expressed. Most translations understandably put the innocence prior to the persecution: "although he had done no violence." Strictly speaking, the verb does not say "had done"; ʿāśâ is in the ordinary perfect tense of past action. There is no pluperfect in biblical Hebrew, though context often requires one in translation, and it is perhaps appropriate here. However, we have noticed that the force of the conjunction ʿal [ʾăšer] is unclear; the line can be read as another affirmation that the servant did and spoke no evil in response to his persecution, as in verse 7. Our translation, with "yet" and the ordinary past tense, is meant to leave this possibility open, while not excluding the meaning that he had not (ever) done wrong.

The servant's innocence is expressed succinctly: he did no violence and he spoke no deceit. These are precisely the evils that characterize the wicked in Micah 6:12.[91] Violence is also the archetypal sin in the Genesis narrative of its entry into the world (Gen. 6:11); and honesty in speech is one of the hallmarks of the righteous person (Job 31:5; Pss. 15:2–4; 24:4) and a well-functioning society (Jer. 9:2–9 [1–8]). Isaiah 53:9b is a compact summary of innocence, embracing both speech and action. Innocence in speech, in biblical thought, also implies innocence in the heart of the person (Luke 6:45).

The statement of innocence in Isaiah 53:9b is formally negative: "he did not do . . . he did not utter . . ." It is not said that

---

90. So Clines, *I, He, We, and They*, 20; also Goldingay, *Message of Isaiah 40–55*, 509; see also NASB. LXX has *hoti*, "because."

91. "Violence" is *ḥāmās* in both texts; "deceit" is *mirmâ* in Isa. 53:9 and the similar *rəmiyyâ* in Mic. 6:12. Micah also has *šeqer*, the regular term for falsehood.

he went about doing good. This fits with the servant's portrait so far in the poem: he has been on the receiving end of extreme abuse, without responding in kind. In his afflictions, "he said not a word" (v. 7). It is close to Jesus's teaching that one should "turn the other cheek" when treated with insult and aggression, rather than taking revenge (Matt. 5:39). This is not passivity. The self-control required to resist evil, both from outside and within oneself, is powerful. It stands against that corruption of the human heart that is at the root of all evil (Gen. 6:5). Negative formulation, as also in the Ten Commandments (Exod. 20:1–17), recognizes the enormous forces that press upon a person to do wrong. To resist such forces implies a turning around of the whole human story. Negative formulations also open up possibilities of renewal. Jesus's Sermon on the Mount shows how a profound reconstruction of all of life can flow from the radical rejection of the determined self-seeking that is sin (Matt. 5–7). It is intriguing to note that Jesus's sermon begins with "He opened his mouth and taught them" (5:2). This contrasts with the saying about the servant: "He said not a word" (or "he opened not his mouth," Isa. 53:7). The echo may be accidental; but it suggests that the power of the servant's silence is unleashed in the life and teaching of Jesus.

Afterthought on 53:7–9

These verses are no longer expressly spoken by the "we" group who have given us our picture of the servant in verses 1–6. They have not disappeared; rather, their voice blends into the overall perspective of the poem, and the thought continues seamlessly.

This short section gives us one of the poem's memorable images, of the lamb led to the slaughter. It is used to highlight the motif of the servant's silence. Until now it has simply been a fact of the poem's expression; but now, with the repeated "he said not a word," it is drawn out as a key element in the servant's bearing of his fate.

The servant's silence corresponds to a further feature of these verses: a heightened sense of his utter isolation. This isolation is not merely a misfortune, a squeamish reluctance of people to be associated with one so visibly marked by affliction; rather, it is a deliberate expulsion, a driving out. This is patent, even if the "cutting off" and the making of his grave are not quite conclusive on whether he died. It was done by a "corruption of justice." We cannot help thinking of the trumped-up charges brought against Jesus by the authorities in his day, who were resolved to eliminate him by any means. The servant is deliberately consigned to utter rejection, exclusion, and aloneness. In his silence he is condemned to silence. The point is closely related to the fact that he suffered "for us." It is part of the "exchange" that places "us," "the many," on one side of the balance and him on the other. The connection between silence/abandonment and the "for us" will be taken up again in chapter 4 of this book, when we consider further the nature of vicarious suffering in terms of the concepts of "representation" and "substitution."

Finally, the servant's innocence is highlighted. This had been implied in the exchange so clearly spelled out in verse 5. Now it becomes an indispensable element in the contrast between the servant and others. The servant is the helpless, innocent lamb in the teeth of ravening wolves.

Isaiah 53:10–12: From Death to Life

In these final verses the poet's lens shifts decisively away from death and toward life. The "life" or "soul" (*nepeš*) of the servant is mentioned in each of these three verses. Out of the shadow of his death comes the prospect of a future, not just for himself but for "many" who are to come after him. His self-sacrificial suffering has had a purpose in the mind of the LORD, and the benefits of it will come to unnumbered people, stretching into the future.

53:10

wyhwh ḥāpēṣ dakkə'ô heḥĕlî   'im-tāśîm 'āšām napšô
But it was the LORD whose will it was to crush and torment him;   when his life is made a guilt offering,

yir'eh zera' ya'ărîk yāmîm   wəḥēpeṣ yhwh bəyādô yiṣlāḥ
he will see offspring and prolong his days,   and the will of the LORD will prosper by him.

Verse 10 is framed by "the will of the LORD," which is in focus in the first and final half-lines. The LORD's purpose in the suffering of his servant was introduced in verse 6 and is now developed. The verse's opening phrase, *wyhwh ḥāpēṣ*, draws attention to the LORD's will by leading with *wyhwh*, "and/but the LORD." When the subject is placed before the verb in Hebrew, as in this case, it puts the subject into focus: the verse will have the LORD's will as its dominant idea. A word-by-word translation would be "and/but the LORD was pleased"; our translation attempts to capture the emphasis given to the LORD. The effect is to affirm that the servant's life and suffering were not random; they were not accidental, nor accounted for merely by human cruelty—even though this was entirely instrumental in it. The servant's suffering had meaning in a scheme of things that is yet to be disclosed. The point of this is missed if the agency of the LORD in the servant's suffering is turned into some philosophical conundrum about the origins of evil. There is some irony in the idea that the LORD had afflicted him. This was exactly what the "we" speakers had formerly thought, before they were converted to a deeper understanding and came to see the error of their old view (v. 4). We noticed that verse 4 did not clarify what the converted group thought about divine punishment in general, and also that LXX avoided the idea. LXX now pointedly leans away both from divine punishment and from the idea that the servant's suffering atoned for sin. For the Greek translators, the LORD wanted only to "cleanse" the servant from his affliction; they also remove from him the responsibility for atonement for sin and lay it at the feet of an unspecified plural addressee, "you." The issue becomes a matter of these hearers' obedience. The thought is elliptical: if only they would "give for sin," their soul would see their offspring have long life, and the LORD would wish to forgive.[92] LXX is evidently responding in a distinctive way to issues that it saw arising from the text before it.

In the Hebrew poem, however, it transpires that the LORD had indeed afflicted the servant. The converts' mistake was in thinking that the servant deserved to be punished by God; now it is plain that his agonies were entirely unmerited. The LORD did indeed will to afflict him. The poem does not discuss this in a philosophical way. Rather, it is a matter of the LORD's perspective on the servant's condition. The LORD's own purpose is somehow being taken forward through the suffering of this innocent man.

The first half-line of verse 10 reiterates the servant's afflictions. According to the LORD's purpose, he would be crushed

---

92. *Ean dōte peri hamartias, hē psuchē humōn opsetai sperma makrobion; kai bouletai kurios aphelein*: "If you [plural] give for sin, your soul will see long-lived offspring/posterity; and the Lord will desire to forgive."

(*dakkə'ô*), recalling verse 5 (*mədukkā'*), and made sick or perhaps brought to grief or torment (*heḥĕlî*).[93] The second halfline brings in two further new dimensions: it begins to suggest the servant's own agency in his fate (which becomes clearer in v. 12); and it calls his selfless action "a guilt offering."

As so often, the linguistic expression of these things needs close inspection. We have translated *'im-tāśîm 'āšām napšô* with "when his life is made a guilt offering." The first word, *'im*, is usually "if," but is taken here as "when" because the clause evidently refers to something that is a given in the context: he has indeed suffered and, by implication, died. The second word, *tāśîm*, could mean "you [second-person masculine singular] made" or "she/it [third-person feminine singular] made"—just another quirk of Hebrew grammar! In our translation we have taken "his life" (the feminine noun *napšô*) as the subject: "his life makes a guilt offering," which is in effect "his life is made a guilt offering." This modifies the idea of the LORD's agency in the servant's death and tends to support the servant's own willing acquiescence in it.[94] Such willing agreement will be borne out in verse 12.

93. The terms used to express his afflictions require comment. The form *dakkə'ô* is infinitive construct piel of *dākâ*, "crush." One would expect the prefixed form *lədakkə'ô* following *ḥāpēṣ*. For *dakkə'ô*, LXX has *katharisai*, apparently reading a form of *zkh* or *zkk*, "purify," rather than *dkh*, "crush." But MT's echo of *mədukkā'*, v. 5, should be preferred. The form *heḥĕlî* is third masculine singular perfect hiphil, "he made sick, weak." Read as such, it is syntactically disjointed. Among various suggestions for improvement is to read it as an infinitive absolute following the infinitive construct form *dakkə'ô* (Clines, *I, He, We, and They*, 20; Koole, *Isaiah III/2*, 320). 1QIsaᵃ, perhaps puzzled by the word, varies with a form of *ḥll*, "pierce."

94. Interpreters ancient and modern have found the word *tāśîm* difficult and proposed emendations. Some have expressed a clear passive sense: "his life/soul was made" (Syr.). Others make the servant the subject. Vg. has *si posuerit pro peccato animam suam*, "if he would give his [own] life for sins." Some modern exegetes read, for example, *hû' śām*, "he made [his life an offering]," or, ingeniously, *'ĕmet śām*, "in truth he made [his life an offering]," which only slightly readjusts the consonants of *'im tāśîm* (*'m tśym* to *'mt śm*). For these and other suggestions, see Koole, *Isaiah III/2*, 322. The tendency of all these is to bring out the agency of the servant more strongly.

If *tāśîm* were rendered "you made," the address would almost certainly be to the LORD: "When you [O LORD] made his life an offering . . ." This could follow logically from the statement of the LORD's agency in the preceding line. Yet there is no other direct address to the LORD in the poem, and a switch from the third to the second person here would be awkward. (It is unlikely to be an address to some other person, such as an enemy, since no such individual has appeared in the poem; and the guilty parties in vv. 1–6 were those who speak as "we.")

The second half-line begins with "when," and in order to complete the sense one must read on into the next full line of the verse. "When his life is made a guilt offering, [then] he will see offspring and prolong his days." The word *'āšām* ("sin, guilt, guilt offering") appears in some contexts that are not strictly sacrificial. It can simply mean "sin" or "guilt" (e.g., Jer. 51:5; Ps. 68:21 [22]). The Philistine king Abimelech complains that Isaac has risked bringing guilt (*'āšām*) on Abimelech by pretending that Rebekah is his sister (Gen. 26:10). At times, the idea of an appeasing gift is to the fore. When Israel's Philistine enemies desperately want to return the ark of the covenant after it had fallen into their hands but proved too hot to handle, they send it back along with an offering (*'āšām*, 1 Sam. 6:3–18, esp. vv. 3–4). The underlying ideas are in the realm of debt and compensation. The guilt offering (*'āšām*) was one of the sacrifices that could be made for sin. When an Israelite incurred guilt, he could make a "guilt offering" so that it might be atoned for (Lev. 5:15–16, 18–19). The offenses in Leviticus 5:15–19 relate to some deficiency in what is due to the LORD ("the holy things of the LORD"), and such deficiency can be valued and compensated for by means of a fitting sacrificial offering. The idea can be applied not only to faults strictly in the realm of worship but also to cases of fraud against a neighbor, which are likewise regarded as sins against the LORD (Lev. 6:1–7 [5:20–26]; Num. 5:6–8). In these cases, the neighbor must be compensated, with a fifth of the value added, and a sacrifice also brought.[95]

The concept of the guilt offering is now applied, astonishingly, to the life of the servant. The noun *'āšām* appears only here in the book of Isaiah,[96] as if called forth by the extraordinary impact the servant has made. In sacrificial contexts it is the animal that is the *'āšām* (e.g., Lev. 5:15, 18–19). So it is striking that, here, it is the servant himself who becomes an "offering," something that is not said of any other human being in the Old Testament. He gave his life, or soul (*napšô*), as this offering. The gift of himself embraces all that he endured while alive and, because of the sacrificial analogy, also his death. Since the *'āšām* is understood as restitution or compensation, it may be asked what the servant's life and death compensate for. As we have seen, the poem has developed the idea of an exchange: the suffering of the innocent servant had the effect that the guilty were spared (Isa. 53:4–6, 9). It is easy to see how the notion of sacrifice is suggested by this motif.

Yet we must be careful not to run hastily to an unwarranted conclusion about what was involved in this. The poem draws on a concept from the sacrificial realm in order to speak about the servant's willing gift of his life for the sake of others. It was not, however, an actual sacrifice.[97] We do not have to imagine

---

95. There are instances of the "guilt offering" that do not readily fit into this typology of compensation, as in the ritual cleansing of a leper (Lev. 14:1–32) or the case of a man who has sex with a slave woman, not knowing she is betrothed (Lev. 19:20–22). The full connotations of biblical sacrifices and the language for them are somewhat elusive.

96. The verb *'āšēm* also occurs once, in Isa. 24:6.

97. For this reason, some prefer the translation "restitution" to "guilt offering" here (e.g., CEB). Yet it seems hard to avoid the implication of sacrifice in a context that bespeaks a death on behalf of others. The objection that the servant could not be offered as a sacrifice because he was physically blemished (Schipper, "Interpreting the Lamb Imagery") is overly literalistic.

him dragged to an altar and ritually slaughtered. Misguided too is the question "To whom was this sacrifice made?" The error of such a literal approach to the idea of sacrifice in Christian atonement theology was recognized long ago by Saint Anselm.[98] Rather, the single appearance in the poem of this concept of a compensatory offering is an element in its rhetorical armory, giving vivid expression to the costliness of the servant's acquiescence. To understand what the servant's suffering effected, we have to consider the poem's full symbolic range. Not least, the sacrificial concept must be placed alongside that of "making righteous" (v. 11). The topic will be returned to more fully in chapter 4, below.

As a parting shot on this, it is interesting that the sage of Proverbs 14:9 wrote, "Fools mock *'āšām*."[99] The converts who speak in Isaiah 53:1–6 no doubt regarded their former selves as foolish. There can be contempt for the folly of self-sacrifice for the sake of others. This also the servant endured.

The "when" clause that began in the first line continues in verse 10b with surprising statements about the servant's continuing life: he will see offspring and live for a long time. How can this be, after the intimations of his death in verses 8–10a? At this point it is well to remember that the poem is capable of being read in different ways. If the servant is understood collectively, as Israel or a portion of it, his life after death can be taken metaphorically to mean renewed life for Israel after the "death" of exile, rather like the image of dry bones amazingly coming to life in Ezekiel 37:1–14. Yet the poem has vividly portrayed the suffering of an individual. The notion of a person living again

---

98. Gunton, *Actuality of Atonement*, 88. The point is important because Anselm's highly influential treatment in *Cur Deus Homo* tended to use legal language in its interpretation of the atonement.

99. The text of Prov. 14:9a is admittedly difficult (*'ĕwilîm yālîṣ 'āšām*), but it is usually taken to mean that fools mock either the idea of sin itself or the idea of making amends for it.

after death is so contrary to expectation and experience that some have found a solution in the supposition that he did not actually die (as we have noted above). Alternatively, it may be argued that the servant's seeing of offspring is not literal, but simply means that he will have followers well into the future. Yet the text does not readily comply with these rationalizations. It is a mistake, as I have argued, to try to map its "narrative" of the servant onto some imagined historical person's life, for it persistently refuses to be constrained in this way. In the most natural reading of it, the servant dies and the servant lives again. It makes no apology and offers no mitigation. The book of Isaiah has elsewhere proposed to us the strangeness of the LORD's work (28:21) and has also spoken of a swallowing up of death forever (25:8). On 53:10, Claus Westermann has wisely written that God's restoration of the servant "is an act done upon him after death, and on the far side of the grave"; and regarding the nature of his death and exaltation, "the text . . . draws a line here, and exegesis ought not to overstep it."[100]

By the same token, we should not reduce the seeing of offspring or the prolonging of days to rational historical meanings. It would go beyond the text to suppose that the historical servant went on to have children and lived a long life in ordinary terms. The resurrected servant's offspring may be those who have followed him, perhaps to be identified with the "servants" first introduced in Isaiah 54:17. That text implies that the mission of the servant finds continuance in those who take him as their example and mentor, who stand in the tradition of the converts who spoke as "we" in 53:1–6, and through whom Israel will be transformed.

The final half-line reverts to the thought with which verse 10 began: that the servant's fate was willed by the LORD. By the

---

100. Westermann, *Isaiah 40–66*, 267.

end of the verse, we have a fuller sense of the servant's willing participation in the purpose for which his life has been lived. It is "by him" or, strictly, "by his hand," that the LORD's will is to be accomplished. In Isaiah, we know that the LORD's will is to redeem Israel and, through Israel, to bring "light to the nations." This has been articulated especially in relation to the servant (Isa. 42:6; 49:6). At the beginning of our poem, in 52:13, the LORD presented his servant as the one whom he would exalt and who would prosper (or "be wise," *yaśkîl*). We now know that the way to this prospering (*yiṣlāḥ*) would be as hard as it could be: through the servant's willing suffering and death.

53:11

mēʿămal napšô yirʾeh   yiśbāʿ bədaʿtô
Out of the trouble of his soul he will see [light];   he will be satisfied by his knowledge.

yaṣdîq ṣaddîq ʿabdî lārabbîm   waʿăwōnōtām hûʾ yisbōl
My servant, the righteous one, will make many righteous; he will shoulder their sins.

In verse 10, the servant assented to be the one through whom the LORD's purpose would be achieved. In verse 11, his role is said once again to be the bearing of the sins of others, recalling verse 5, now with the added nuance of "making many righteous."

While the portrait of the servant has hitherto largely consisted of what was done to him by others, we are now given a glimpse into his subjective experience. In the first phrase, *mēʿămal napšô*, it seems appropriate to translate *napšô* (*nepeš*)

as "soul" rather than "life," as rendered in verse 10, hence "out
of the trouble of his soul." The reader in Hebrew sees only the
same word in each case, and one should not imagine an absolute
difference between "life" and "soul." In verse 10, *nepeš* simply
denoted the servant's life and its loss culminating in death.
In verse 11, his life is viewed in terms of its inner vitality, the
person's subjectivity. The idea of "soul" does not imply some
separable part of the human constitution. There is no dualism
in the Old Testament between the physical and the spiritual;
life and soul are simply aspects of the same reality. The use of
"soul" in English, therefore, implies no dualism, but rather
attempts to penetrate to the heart of a person's being. One
might compare the first line of Psalm 103: "Bless the LORD, O
my soul [*napšî*], and all that is within me, bless his holy name"
(NRSV, ESV). In some contexts, *nepeš* can simply stand for the
self, without an implication of the depths in a person, and in
such cases it can be passed over in translation or rendered as
"oneself." This underlies NRSV's rendering of *mēʿămal napšô*
in our verse as "out of his anguish" (where *napšô* is rendered by
"his"). However, in the present instance the poetic line draws
attention to the servant's inner life, and it is best to give fuller
value to the word. The word *ʿămal* can mean "burdensome
toil," as in Ecclesiastes 2:18, but often implies serious trouble
or distress (e.g., Judg. 10:16; Ps. 73:5) or even mischief made by
the wicked (Job 15:35). The servant knew trouble, or anguish,
of soul. While his physical abuse and ostracization were on
public view, there was an inner anguish that could not be seen
and whose depth might not be known.

His inner turmoil, however, produces something new. Its
good outcomes are also couched in subjective terms: "he will
see," "he will be satisfied." The statement that "he will see"
is surprisingly laconic. What will he see? The Hebrew of MT

supplies no object, nothing that is "seen." However, both the Isaiah Scroll from Qumran (1QIsaᵃ) and LXX add "light," a combined testimony that strongly suggests it may well have been part of the original text. Among modern translations, NRSV and NIV follow this line, the latter expanding to "the light of life." There is no certainty in such cases. However, "light" is not an unexpected answer to the question "What will the servant see?" It is a major metaphor for salvation in the book of Isaiah (e.g., 9:2 [1]), and elsewhere for life itself (e.g., Ps. 49:19 [20]; Job 3:16). In relation to the servant's experience, it occurs in Isaiah 50:10, where he is said to trust in the LORD even though he "walks in darkness and has no light." The idea in our text, that he sees light as a result of the anguish he has experienced, gains strength from this statement that he had previously walked without light.

There is cogency, however, in the mere idea of the servant's "seeing," especially when paired with "knowledge" in the following half-line. Together with hearing and understanding, seeing is a marked concept in Isaiah, ever since the enigmatic 6:9–10. We have already noted this in commenting on Isaiah 52:15, where it was said that kings would see and understand things they had not previously heard. Seeing and understanding are essential to the LORD's purpose for Israel. Just as the moral failure that had placed them under God's judgment could be characterized as *not* seeing, hearing, and understanding, so seeing and understanding stand for the moral transformation that would bring Israel back into fellowship with the LORD. In the underlying narrative of the book of Isaiah, Israel undergoes the purging caused by defeat and oppression by powerful enemies. Here, more remarkably, the servant is said to have come to see and understand after a harrowing experience of his own. The MT form of the text, without the expressed object "light," has the virtue of focusing closely on this inner experience of the servant.

Not only will he see, but he will be satisfied, another pointer to the subjective aspect of his ordeal. In the line as we have set it out in the translation, following *BHS*, "he will be satisfied" is joined closely to "by his knowledge" (*bəda'tô*). It is also possible that "by his knowledge" belongs with the following line, thus: "By his knowledge my servant, the righteous one, will make many righteous." There is support for the latter option in the MT's punctuation.[101] Many modern readers favor this, though a minority voice aligns with *BHS* and our own translation (e.g., NRSV). The question for interpreters is whether the servant was satisfied by his knowledge, or whether it was by his knowledge that he made many righteous.

The balance may be tipped by the parallelism of "seeing" and "knowledge" that is produced by the line-form adopted here, since they belong within the same conceptual field. Along with "wisdom," "understanding," and "seeing," "knowledge" is a key term in Isaiah's moral and religious repertoire.[102] As the servant comes to see, so he comes to know. He has come, through his experience, to a profound grasp of the purpose of the LORD for Israel, the nations, and himself.

The idea that the innocent servant should come to a new depth of understanding through his trauma is striking. He has been portrayed in the poem as acting and suffering on behalf of others. Yet here his own possession of insight and knowledge is in view. It may help, once again, to think of the multivalency of the servant paradigm. Though an individual, he does not cease to be a type of the renewed, ideal Israel. At this point, his acquisition of knowledge through suffering has a parallel

101. MT puts the punctuation mark *zāqēp parvum* above *yiśbā'*, signifying the end of a sense unit at that word.

102. See, e.g., Isa. 5:13; 11:2; 40:14; 44:19, 25.

in the purging of Israel through exile, whose aim was to restore the people to righteousness (Isa. 1:21–26).

In this light, the servant's knowledge can be understood to have a connection with his role in making many righteous. Perhaps we can think of *bəda'tô*, "by his knowledge," as having a kind of Janus quality, looking both backward and forward, an idea that finds some support from the hesitation in the transmission of the text about how it should be laid out. This idea also finds support in the drift of the poem to this point. The poet has made it plain that the servant's suffering has been for the sake of others; there has been an exchange between what has befallen the innocent servant and the escape of guilty people from what they came to see as their just desert. The present verse extends the thought: the knowledge that he acquires through his suffering becomes the ground on which he can bring others to righteousness.

Righteousness is the key idea in the next phrase, highlighted by the succession of the words *yaṣdîq ṣaddîq*, both related to *ṣədāqâ*, "righteousness." Together with *'abdî*, "my servant," the phrase means "my servant, the righteous one [*ṣaddîq*], will make righteous [*yaṣdîq*]." The thought is completed with *lārabbîm*, "[the] many."[103] The epithet *ṣaddîq* is applied generally to righteous people, with Noah and Abraham as paradigms (Gen. 6:9; 18:19),[104] and occasionally to the LORD (Deut. 32:4; Ps. 119:137). It is not surprising that it should be attributed to the servant in view of his innocence and his close alignment with the LORD's underlying purpose to bring justice to the world (Isa. 42:1) and light to the nations (42:6; 49:6). The

---

103. The form *lārabbîm* is the object of "make righteous"; the prefixed *lə* is typically a preposition, but it functions here as the sign of a definite object, as also in 2 Sam. 3:30. The form is strictly "*the* many."

104. In Abraham's case the LORD says that he has chosen him to teach his descendants "justice and righteousness" (*ṣədāqâ ûmišpāṭ*).

servant is not only innocent of whatever accusations may have been made against him, but he is an exemplar of righteousness (*ṣədāqâ*). This foundational Old Testament concept embraces honesty, integrity, and a right disposition toward others. But it is no mere static ethical quality; rather, it is active and transformative. This is evident in its application to the servant and has immense implications.

It is clear that the servant's making many righteous is an action that changes things. The scope of this transformation can be inferred partly from within the poem, since the LORD has from the outset drawn the attention of nations and rulers to his servant, and declares that they will be dumbstruck because of him (Isa. 52:13–15). From the wider book of Isaiah, we know that the LORD acts on the largest canvas of history, bringing down haughty powers (2:6–21; 10:5–19). In this context, Jerusalem was a city in which "righteousness" (*ṣedeq*) dwelt and would dwell again, a visible symbol of a rightly ordered world (1:21–26; 2:2–4). What needs to be transformed is nothing less than the whole world, the LORD's creation, which lies ruined under the LORD's judgment (Isa. 24). The conflict in which sinful humanity is involved is with Death itself, with its power to destroy and corrupt (25:6–10a; 28:14–21). When the righteous servant makes many righteous, he does so at the heart of the deepest disturbances in heaven and earth.

But how is the servant to "make many righteous"? One important sense of the phrase "make righteous," employing the same verbal form as here (*yaṣdîq* or *hiṣdîq*), is to declare someone innocent, as in a courtroom setting (e.g., Deut. 25:1; Isa. 5:23). Yet this idea hardly seems adequate in the present context. The servant has not been portrayed as a judge who stands outside a case that is brought before him. Another possible model is in Daniel 12:3, where the phrase "and those who turn many to righteousness" (*ûmaṣdîqê hārabbîm*) formally resembles the one in our text.[105] The Daniel text refers to a kind of leadership or instruction by those who are "wise," which has a certain echo of the servant's "knowledge." Yet this also does not fully express the servant's role. Not merely a teacher, he has been totally involved, with pain and sacrifice of body and soul, in a work that has been laid on him by the Lord. "Out of the trouble of his soul" he has come to "see" and has attained "knowledge." The servant's righteousness can hardly be disentangled from this severe education. It is the righteousness of the innocent sufferer who has endured the worst that can befall a human being. In the progress of the Lord's plan for his servant, it is only now that he declares that he will make others righteous.

Does he achieve this simply by his example? From the testimony of the speakers in verses 1–6, we know that the servant made a deep impact on them and that they had been transformed in their attitude to him. It is reasonable to think that their conversion went deeper than a mere recognition of a misperception and led them to become followers, with perhaps radical changes of thought and deed. We have observed already that after the servant of chapters 41–53 come the "servants," first named in 54:17, who appear in due course to become victims of persecution within the postexilic community of Judah, albeit ultimately vindicated.[106] If this is what is entailed by "making [many] righteous," it has obvious similarities with Jesus's call to his disciples to take up their cross and follow him.[107] This explanation of "making righteous" depends on the powerful, transformative influence of a compelling personality, one who

105. The form *ûmaṣdîqê* is, like *yaṣdîq*, a hiphil (causative) part of the verb *ṣādaq*, but in a participial form.
106. This seems to be the implication of texts like Isa. 63:15–19; 65:13–15.
107. Matt. 16:24–26; Mark 8:34–35; Luke 9:23–25.

has so captivated people that they will follow him anywhere. And the servant's influence is now seen to extend not only to those who confessed in 53:1–6 but to "many." The servant's impact on "many" was already declared in 52:14a, 15a, and specified as "many nations" in the latter case. It is hardly an accident that, as the poem draws to its climax, there should be an echo of its opening: the impact of the servant's life is felt not just in a small local environment, but will be far-reaching. The first hearers of the poem may have understood who the "many" in 53:11 were. They may have been the people of Jerusalem and Judah, enriched by the return of Babylonian exiles; or the term may be influenced by the "many nations" of 52:15, which would push this text in a universal direction. For the modern reader, the reference is opaque; as so often, the poem draws a line for the interpreter, beyond which little can be said. Nor does "many" necessarily refer to the same group throughout the poem. The "many nations" who are stunned into silence in 52:15 may be quite different from the "many" who are made righteous in 53:11. In fact, in these closing verses of the poem, the idea of "many" becomes a motif, as we shall also see in verse 12. The servant's relation to the "many" takes several forms. The motif has one unmistakable effect, however: it creates a powerful contrast with the image of the servant in the body of the poem as one completely cut off from human society, one who endured the attempt to extinguish his life and memory. If there were those who wished this, their plot was doomed to rebound badly. The servant's life would not be hidden in some dark place, but would burst forth with immeasurable benefits for untold numbers of people. The openness of the idea of the "many" will reverberate into the New Testament and beyond.

Yet the "exemplary" explanation can hardly account for the final phrase in the line: "he will shoulder their sins [*waʿăwōnōtām hû' yisbōl*]." The verb "shoulder," *yisbōl*, we last met in verse 4 in the phrase "[it was] our pains that he shouldered." (The verb effectively means the same as "bear"; "shoulder" was chosen at v. 4 for the sake of variety in the line, which also contained *nāśā'*, "bear, lift up.") Whereas in verse 4 it was "our pains" that the servant shouldered, here it is "their sins." There are two important differences. The scope has widened from "our" to "their," now referring to the "many" who are to be made righteous. And it is now "sins" themselves that the servant has taken upon himself. When we were considering in what sense the servant was said to have suffered *for* others in verses 4–6, 8, we found that the idea of his vicarious suffering emerged in the course of the poem. This last half-line of verse 11 contributes strongly to that impression. The word for sin here is *'āwōn*, which can denote not only sin itself but its consequences in guilt and punishment. To say that the servant "shouldered" or "bore" their sins implies that he also took their consequences. They sinned, and the punishment fell on him.

It is worth noting that the form of the line (v. 11b) accentuates this point. It has two basic propositions: that the servant will make many righteous and that he will shoulder their sins. But the second of these is structured so as to emphasize that *he* has done this. The pronoun *hû'*, "he," is not strictly necessary for the sense, but highlights his agency. It was he who did this, and no one else.

Verse 11 became vitally important for the New Testament writers in their proclamation of Jesus. The apostle Paul took up the idea of a righteous one making many righteous in his teaching about justification through faith in Jesus (Rom. 5:18–19). Just as the Hebrew underlines the connection between the servant's righteousness and those he makes righteous by means of the verbal echo in *yaṣdîq ṣaddîq*, so too does Paul in his phrase "through the righteous act of one, the making righteous of many" (Rom. 5:18).[108] Paul's play with words in the field of *dikaios*, "righteous" (*dikaiōmatos . . . dikaiōsin*), is often not evident in translations: NRSV is typical with "by the one man's *obedience* the many will be made righteous" (5:19). This reflects the specific meaning of the word *dikaiōma*, which in the context probably means "righteous act" and contrasts with the first man Adam's act of disobedience. Yet for Paul, the *dikaios* word-field is supremely important.[109] His sense of what constitutes "righteousness" is enmeshed in his theological dialogue with other Jewish thinkers of his time. As we noted a moment ago, righteousness in the Old Testament had an active, transformative character. Paul builds on this as he develops his idea that the righteousness conferred by Christ is a saving righteousness before God. The point is strengthened by the addition of the word *zōēs*, "of life," in Romans 5:18, which has no counterpart in Isaiah 53:11. The righteousness that Christ confers on "all" (Rom. 5:18) or "many" (v. 19) is one that leads to "life," by which Paul means eternal life.[110]

The Gospel of Mark also takes up the idea of the "many" and combines it with the bearing of others' sins (Mark 10:45). The allusion there is clearly to the servant of Isaiah, who "bore the sin of many." The "servant" language should also be noticed in the phrase "[he] came not to be served but to serve." Mark applies this, of course, to Jesus. Jesus is actually called the "Son of Man" in this text (Mark 10:45), a title drawn from

108. *Di henos dikaiōmatos eis pantas anthrōpous eis dikaiōsin zōēs.*

109. Paul's insistence on the verbal link in the *dikaios*-field is supported by LXX's juxtaposition of the terms *dikaiōsai* and *dikaion* and is surely intentional. LXX has somewhat recast the line, apparently making the servant ("the just one") the object of the justifying. Paul is using the Greek of LXX, but his thought is closer to MT.

110. Cranfield writes about the text in Rom. 5:19, "This righteous status has life, eternal life, for its result," and compares v. 17 for corroboration (Cranfield, *Epistle to the Romans*, 289).

Daniel (Dan. 7:13), which testifies to how the New Testament writers drew together a variety of Old Testament texts as they proclaimed Jesus's fulfillment of all God's promises. In this context, there would appear to be no limit to the "many"; the idea that it might be bounded by the limits of a national group, for example, is foreign to the Gospels.

The prominence of the idea of the servant's vicarious suffering in the poem is further borne out by its repetition, in slightly different words, in the final line (v. 12b).

53:12

lākēn ʾăḥalleq-lô bārabbîm   wəʾet-ʿăṣûmîm yəḥallēq šālāl
Therefore I will divide him a portion with the many,   and he will share plunder with the strong,

taḥat ʾăšer heʿĕrâ lammāwet napšô   wəʾet-pōšəʿîm nimnâ
in recognition that he poured out his life to death   and allowed himself to be numbered among rebels,

wəhûʾ ḥēṭʾ-rabbîm nāśāʾ   wəlappōšəʿîm yapgîaʿ
though it was he who bore the sin of many   and makes intercession for the rebels.

The poem has a way of surprising us to the very end. This last verse is a ringing declaration of the Lord's favor bestowed on his servant in recognition of what he has done. The poem opened in 52:13, we recall, with the Lord affirming that the servant would "prosper," or "be wise," in what seemed to run counter to the core of the poem. But this final verse now echoes that confident beginning, so that the poem is framed with the perspective that the servant's submission to the Lord's will would end in glorious triumph.

The first line has military connotations, introducing a new kind of metaphor to the poem. To divide a portion and share plunder is to enjoy the spoils of victory, and in this the servant is counted among the "many" and the "strong." The word "many" is striking in this line, highlighting again the flexibility of the motif, because it now denotes powerful victors. Indeed, the word *rabbîm* (singular *rab*) is often better understood as "great" or "mighty," a sense strongly suggested here by its parallel with *ʿaṣûmîm* and consequently adopted by many translations.[111] I have retained "many" in order to draw attention to the frequency of the word in these last two verses. Although it appears again in a quite different sense in the final line of the verse, the poet apparently wants us to notice its recurrence.

But who are these "many/great" and "strong"? To answer this, the whole verse must be taken into account, and especially the two different uses of "many." While the "many" in verse 12a look initially like ordinary victorious warriors, the "many" in verse 12c are the opposite of powerful people, those who required someone else to "bear their sins" and to intercede for them. "Many" does not always have to be the same people, as we have noted. However, the ideas of many victors and many sinners stand in evident tension with each other, and the effect is to suggest a complete rethinking of what it might mean for the servant to share spoils of victory.

Isaiah 40–55 unfolds several stories of victory: of the Persian king Cyrus defeating the oppressive empire of Babylon (Isa. 45:1–3; 48:14–21); of a rebuilt and renewed Zion, who sees her children wonderfully restored to her after years of loss and humiliation (Isa. 54); and of the servant of the LORD, who is restored to life after being given over to death and who "makes

---

111. In military terms, "great" and "many" are not very different, since a great army will also be numerous.

many righteous." It is the servant's victory that is decisive for the others. The return of exiles from Babylon to Jerusalem is according to the LORD's purpose, but not the nub of it. It is the victory of the servant that gives a new sense to victory itself. His sharing of the spoils of battle is a metaphor; he did not actually divide up booty on the field. His is a victory of righteousness; but more than that, it has been won mysteriously through his innocence, in conflict with the darkest forces of injustice and violence.

It is this spiritual conflict that comes back into focus in the remainder of the verse. The phrase "in recognition that" (*taḥat ʾăšer*) is stronger than simply "because," but suggests a kind of balancing or compensation. The servant's reward was a recognition of the kind of victory he had won. He had won it by "pouring out his life to death." The word implies a relinquishment of all defense.[112] He had willingly exposed himself to his fate. The servant's death was alluded to in verse 9, but this is the clearest statement of his own readiness to face it. There is something especially chilling about this exposure to death. The word has resonances beyond ordinary mortality, as we see in the strange passage in Isaiah 28:14–18, in which corrupt leaders in Jerusalem are said to have made "a covenant with death." In that text, death appears as a kind of terrible power. In Canaanite mythology, death takes the form of the god Mot, a destructive force that opposes life and order. This is the sense in which the "covenant with death" should be understood in Isaiah 28:15, 18.[113] The point is reinforced by its parallel phrase

---

112. The form *heʿĕrâ* is a hiphil of *ʿārâ*, "be bare," and so can mean "lay bare," as in texts about sexual offenses (e.g., Lev. 20:18; see also Isa. 3:17). This would make sense in our text (and is so taken by JPS/NJPS). The meaning "poured out" is found in niphal form in Isa. 32:15 and is favored by most translations.

113. Linguistically, the Hebrew word for death, *māwet*—or, consonantally, *môt*—is the same as the Canaanite Mot.

in those verses, "agreement with Sheol"; Sheol is the underworld or place of the dead, personified here as a lethal agent. It is to Death as a terrible, ruthless enemy that the servant gave himself up.

The servant is now said to have "allowed himself to be numbered among rebels."[114] This is a new angle in the poem. The word "rebels" is *pōšə'îm*, a verbal participle meaning "those who rebel." The servant has previously been depicted as having been "wounded because of our rebelliousness" (v. 5), using the closely related noun *peša'* (*mippəšā'ēnû*). Up till now, however, the sins have been on the other side of the equation from the servant; in his innocence, he suffered for their sins. But now there is a new intimation of solidarity. The servant had somehow been counted in with "sinners." In what way this was so, the poem does not reveal. One could imagine some scenario in which he was reckoned to be part of a dissident group that was persecuted. The poem allows us to indulge in such imagination, but, as usual, one cannot turn it into a compelling narrative. It is more convincing simply to suppose that, when he was suspected and maligned, he made no protest or defense, like the lamb led silently to the slaughter (v. 7). Although the servant is plainly exonerated from complicity in the sins or rebelliousness for which he paid the price, he has willingly stood alongside the sinners.

The last line underlines this point. Yes, he was counted along with sinners *even though* it was he who bore the sin of many: he stood with sinners even though he had taken the burden of their sin upon himself and relieved them from it. The motif of exchange is pursued to the last, and here with a new edge. The word *ḥēṭ'* occurs here for the first time in the poem. It can

114. The word *nimnâ* is a niphal form of *mānâ*, "to count," which could have a passive sense ("he was counted"). But the more self-involving connotation reflected in our translation suits the context of the servant's willing self-giving.

carry the sense of a fault or omission, as in Genesis 41:9, but in Isaiah it is one of the stock terms for Israel's sin (as in Isa. 1:18). Crucial here is the phrase "bear sin," because it is at home in the sphere of incurring guilt and becoming liable to punishment.[115] Normally, it is the sinners themselves who bear the responsibility for their own sin. But here, extraordinarily, it is the servant who bears it for others. That the servant suffered vicariously for the sins of others is unmistakable here.

He bore the sins of *many*. The thought is familiar and yet slightly new. We already know that he "was wounded because of *our* rebelliousness" (v. 5), and also that his mission is to "make many righteous" (v. 11); but only now is his bearing of sin explicitly said to be for the many. The progression from "us" to "many" is striking. The broad canvas on which the servant's effect was announced at the beginning (52:13, 15) is reaffirmed at the end. There is no limit to the benefits he has won.

It is striking that when Jesus quotes the line "he allowed himself to be numbered among rebels" (Luke 22:37), he takes it in an unexpected way, apparently to underscore the danger to him from sinners—and therefore danger to his disciples—as he approached his destiny on earth.[116] Crucially, he identifies himself with the servant's fate and implies an analogy between the LORD's purpose for the servant and the LORD's purpose for himself.

In a final twist, the lens reverts to the "rebels." The verse actually interleaves "many" and "rebels" in an ABAB pattern. The effect is to keep in view both the wide scope of the servant's work and the sense that it somehow covered guilt. The alternating

---

115. For *nāśā'ḥēt'* as "incur guilt," "be subject to punishment," or "bear the consequences of sin," see Lev. 19:17; 20:20; 24:15; Ezek. 23:49.

116. As Nolland puts it, "It seems best to take the quotation as concerned only to evoke more generally the prospect of the violent fate anticipated for the figure in Isa 52–53" (Nolland, *Luke 18:35–24:53*, 1077).

pattern of "many" and "rebels" is not static, however, but shows progression and novelty. In the concept of "rebels" the note of a moral struggle is sustained to the end. Can the guilt of rebels easily be assuaged? The servant's last recorded act is to "intercede" for the rebels. The concept presupposes their danger. A captured rebel might be subject to dire punishment, which only a powerful mediator might manage to turn aside. The danger to the rebel might, however, come from God, in which case the intercessor could be none other than a prophet. In Jeremiah's time, when the Lord had resolved to punish Judah, he forbade the prophet from carrying out one of his appointed responsibilities, to "intercede" for the people (Jer. 7:16). The same word is used in that case as here of the servant, and the concept is filled out with praying and crying out to the Lord.[117] In spite of his embargo, Jeremiah's whole ministry could be seen as an "intercession" for sinful Judah, exercised with the utmost passion and at great personal cost.[118] So what did intercession look like for the servant? It was evidently more than uttering prayers; rather, his whole obedient self-offering, through extremes of hostility and endurance, is re-presented in this final phrase as an intercession. His whole life and being became an offering for the life of rebels.

Afterthought on 53:10–12

The poem reaches its climax, teeming with new ideas. Typically, it does so with an airy disregard for explanation! The ser-

---

117. Jeremiah is told, 'al-tipga'-bî, "do not intercede to me" (from pāga', qal, "meet, entreat"). The servant will yapgîa' for the rebels, a hiphil imperfect form of the same verb. The hiphil form is infrequent and carries this specific meaning of "intercede" (cf. Jer. 36:25).

118. It is part of the "narrative" of Jeremiah that his intercession was of no effect, that it produced only hostility on the part of his fellow Judeans. The prophet even felt deceived by the Lord; he is not promised success, but only personal deliverance, e.g., Jer. 11:19–20; 15:15–21; 20:7–12.

vant, having been removed from life, lives again. But his afterlife is not mere survival; rather, it is full of purpose. Through him many will become righteous. Here the "exchange" that has characterized the servant's relation to others throughout the poem becomes benign: the righteous one makes righteous. The idea that his suffering might have an intended outcome in great benefits has hitherto lain dormant in the poem, though in retrospect it was signaled in 52:13, with its announcement that the servant would be exalted. Now we are drawn again to the realization that the servant's treatment took place, not in some domestic corner, but in a far bigger theater. Kings would be dumbstruck (52:15)— and many would be made righteous! These two grand claims are correlative. At the outset of the book of Isaiah, it was the LORD's declared intention that the city of Jerusalem should be restored to its former righteousness (1:21–26). Correspondingly, it would be a magnet for the nations, who would flow to it in order to learn from the LORD (2:2–4). Somehow this purpose has been achieved through the paradoxical humiliation/exaltation of the servant. In New Testament reception of the servant's work, his "making many righteous" becomes a way of declaring that a deep corruption in all things has been put right ("righteoused," justified, rectified) through him.

This world-renewing mission has been laid upon the servant by the LORD. It is the will of the LORD that has driven the whole story (Isa. 53:10 [2×]). The LORD chose his servant and placed him before the eyes of the world (52:13). The trajectory from his humiliation to his exaltation is a revelation of the LORD's deep purposes for the world. This raises enormous questions about the way in which God may be thought to be present in history. It also will lead us to the cross of Christ and to a question about tragedy: Must there be suffering so that ultimate good may come? We will return to this in the following chapter.

Finally on these verses, it is essential to observe that it is not only the will of the LORD that operates in the poem, but also the servant's. He "poured himself out for many," in a section that employs sacrificial language about his self-giving. Nor does he stop there; in his renewed life, he "makes intercession" for many. The poem evinces no concern about arbitrariness or unfairness on the part of the LORD. It does not have the form or content of a lament. It poses instead a profound question about the relationship between human suffering, the presence of God in the world, and the conditions necessary for righteousness ultimately to prevail over evil. The willingness of the servant will find its echo in the willingness of Jesus in his anticipation of the cross.

4

The Servant and Christ

Preamble

I have been suggesting throughout that we do not arrive at an imagined definitive meaning of Isaiah 53 by digging it out, as it were, by means of historical and philological tools, indispensable as these are to a rounded understanding. Rather, we have to allow it to speak to us in its own chosen terms. To that end, we have considered Isaiah 53 in some detail in the preceding chapter, paying attention to the ways in which it creates meaning with all the resources available to the poet who composed it. We noticed that it was both extraordinarily powerful in its imagery, yet strangely reticent about certain kinds of questions that might occur to a reader. It can make the boldest of claims, while often avoiding explicit assertion. At its end, much is left open. Where does it lead? What are we to make of it? I now want to pursue a little further our inquiry into how the poem makes meaning.

Isaiah 53 and Its Symbolic World

This entails, first, asking how it sits within the world of ideas that, as far as we can judge, were current when it was written.

To put things another way, what is its "symbolic world"? This question involves searching beneath the surface of the text, looking for the concepts that made up the poet's thought-world. While we cannot actually get inside the poet's mind, there are pointers throughout the Old Testament and within Isaiah to the ways in which his mental world may have been structured. Prominent among these structuring concepts are the one God YHWH (the Lord), enthroned in heaven and reigning on earth from his temple on Mount Zion; Israel as his chosen people, liberated from slavery in Egypt to be in covenant with him, enjoying his gifts of land and prosperity; and the Davidic king as his chosen "son," charged with governing the people of Israel justly. These are visibly represented in the temple and royal palace and in the regular great feasts (Passover, Weeks, and Tabernacles), in which the tribes of Israel gathered three times a year at the temple to symbolize their unity as the people of the Lord. Also important are the powerful ideas of justice and righteousness, which Israel was called to exhibit, and holiness, made visibly present in the community by holy places (chiefly the temple), times (the feasts), people (the priests), and actions (sacrifice).[1] Righteousness and holiness are threatened by sin and its disordering effects, and the holiness apparatus offers ways of restitution through a system of offerings and sacrifices. All of these are sustained in the common memory through narrative, prophecy, psalms, and poetry, as well as by regular enactment in the commemorative actions of the feasts.[2]

These concepts are mostly somewhat muted in Isaiah 53, though at times they break the surface. But there is an important

---

1. These are analyzed carefully by Jenson, *Graded Holiness*.
2. This list is not exhaustive. One might add, for example, wisdom, which was also visibly present in practitioners and texts such as Proverbs; cf. Jer. 18:18.

caveat: the concepts and symbols that form the poet's world are not fixed and immutable. The prophets were continually preoccupied with challenging Israel's misconstruals of some of the formative elements in their identity and vocation, not least their status as the LORD's chosen people. The book of Isaiah brings new vitality to the call to worship the one God YHWH (with its entailment in the vacuity of the gods of Babylon) and grounds this faith in the LORD's sole power over historical events. Davidic messianism also undergoes development in Isaiah, with its so-called democratization (Isa. 55:3), though this sits alongside more conventional messianic cameos in the final book (such as 9:2–7 [1–6]; 11:1–9). I want to suggest that Isaiah 53 also manifests this readiness for innovation in relation to some of the major symbolic building blocks of Israel's world.

God and the Servant: Suffering and Justice

The portrait of the servant in Isaiah 53 leads to the question "In what way is God present in this human situation?" The poem itself invites the question; or rather, the LORD invites it by pointing to "my servant" right at the start (52:13) and declaring that he will have a profound effect on the movements of history ("kings will be dumbstruck because of him," 52:15). We noticed in our exegesis of 52:13 a purposeful alignment of the LORD and the servant.[3] In his exaltation, the servant is like the LORD. The LORD's supremacy over historical events is one of the chief themes of the book of Isaiah. He can raise up mighty kingdoms for a purpose and put them down again to show that he alone is God (Isa. 10:5–34; 40). He can punish and redeem his people by moving empires. What part can be played in this divine mastery of history by a single suffering human figure?

3. Citing Williams, "Another Look at the 'Lifting Up' in the Gospel of John," 62.

The LORD's agency in his servant's suffering is explicit in 53:6, 10, which declare that he willed the servant's sufferings, and also in verse 12, where some accolade is promised to the servant in consequence of his having "made many righteous." This trajectory is woven into the larger fabric of the great weaver's purposes. But how are we to understand it? The question runs from Isaiah 53 through to the atoning life and death of Jesus Christ. Is the servant a helpless, hapless tool in the hands of the mighty God?

This question goes to the heart of the Old Testament's portrayal of how God works in the world, and especially to the nature of his justice. This concern is never far from the minds of the psalmists, for example, in Psalm 73, which is bewildered by the offense to justice in the prosperity of the wicked and how they seem to escape the afflictions common to others (Ps. 73:1–5). It is voiced by Jeremiah in the midst of his own trials (Jer. 12:1b). And it is dramatized at length in the book of Job. It is striking, however, that all these wrestlings are expressed within prayers or, in Job's case, in a prolonged and passionate quest to meet God directly. They are not abstract and intellectualized but come out of a strong sense that, because of the nature of God, there must be some deeper meaning to things than meets the eye. This can be seen in the confessional preambles to protest in Psalm 73:1 and Jeremiah 12:1a, in which the worshiper expresses his underlying faith. Job contests his innocence in dialogue with friends who in various ways imply or declare that he must have committed some offense against God. In their syllogism, "Sin leads to punishment, you are suffering, therefore you are being punished for sin." This was so powerful a concept that it was still prevalent in Jesus's day, as exemplified in the case of the man born blind in John 9. For Job, on the contrary, his innocence is beyond suspicion, and he is driven by the need for God to explain to him how his innocent suffering can be just.

Isaiah 53 takes its place in this search for justice in God's world. Formally, it resists classification. It is not a lament, as no one really laments here. The servant's sufferings are depicted by others. The "we" speakers are implicitly penitent and so might invite comparison with psalms such as 32 and 51. But this does not explain Isaiah 53 as a whole. The LORD himself joins the chorus, not to respond to the human voices but (with them) to place the servant at center stage. As for the servant, he is not simply the object of others' actions. Since he does not speak, we can only infer his own will in the matter. But he offers no resistance to his fate. He is predominantly the subject of verbs in the poem. This does not equate to willing agency, as a number of these verbs are passive. Yet in 53:10–12 there is an implication of agency. The servant is portrayed as an agent in the gift of his life, in bearing others' sins, and in "making intercession for the rebels" (53:12). Whether the same is true of making his life to be "a guilt offering" is uncertain, but verse 10 can be read this way in light of verse 12. Finally, verse 11 focuses on the servant's subjective experience and what he has achieved. Through his anguish, he comes to "see." He finds satisfaction through his knowledge, also acquired (it seems) through his anguish. Crucially, as a correlative of shouldering "their" sin, he—the righteous one—"will make many righteous" (*yaṣdîq ṣaddîq 'abdî lārabbîm*). This outcome of the servant's work places it squarely within that part of the Old Testament literature that seeks to understand the justice of God.

What does this particular witness contribute to that tradition? At the least, it is one of the voices, alongside Job's, that denies the necessary connection between sin and suffering. But it packs a heavier punch than this. The dramatic tension in the poem does not lie in a confrontation between human beings and God. Rather, the divine will and a human will are ranged together against other forces. These forces are not readily named, but they are adumbrated in the kings who find themselves silenced by the servant (52:15). They are present in the dark background in which some untold violence has been done to an innocent man. They are evident in the self-regarding ostracism of the disfigured sufferer by decent society. And they are active and virulent in the willful corruption of justice by which he is condemned. These cumulative offenses against the servant are an assault at the deepest level on truth and justice themselves. The antagonistic powers are personified as Death in Isaiah 28:15, 18. They are met and overcome when a human being willingly submits to their full force. This "will of the Lord" (53:10) runs counter to everything that we may be tempted to imagine as divine power. Would it not be better to invoke fire from heaven against such evils, as Elijah once did (2 Kings 1:9–16), or, like Peter, to unsheathe a sword against those who would arrest Jesus (John 18:10)? In a way that remains hidden and mysterious, evil is confounded by the servant's freely chosen path through it.

Just as the forces of evil lay siege to the greatest goods, truth and justice themselves, so these same things are restored in the outcomes achieved by the servant's submission to his fate. The key is in the "righteous one" who makes many righteous. As we saw in the preceding chapter, in 53:11 the idea of "making righteous" aims at the transformation of the whole creation, a defeat of the forces arrayed against God and his will for truth and justice, and God's ultimate achievement of the rightly ordered world of his creative design. The apostle Paul strikes this note with his image of a creation "subjected to futility" and in "bondage to decay," groaning in pain as it awaits "the freedom of the glory of the children of God" (Rom. 8:19–23 NRSV). This hope is no abstract ideal. Just as Paul maintains a close relationship between the aching creation and the revealing of the children of God, the Isaianic poem knows that the transformation of all things begins with "the many." Their role is to become exemplars of truth and righteousness in the world, with the aim of creating a true and righteous world.[4] This may indeed mean taking up a cross.

Theologically speaking, the point is "incarnational." This is what is at stake in our observation that both the LORD and the servant act as agents in the poem. The unity of will between the LORD and the servant forecloses any notion of God's arbitrary victimization of a human being, or "cosmic child abuse," as some would have it. The restoration of a world in which human beings can find and live their best reality is one that depends on an innocent human being confronting and overcoming, at the cost of his life, the forces of hatred and death.

The idea of a transformed creation has extensions into Christian atonement theology. For Colin Gunton, atonement is a reordering of a disordered creation. What is at stake, in words borrowed from Saint Anselm, is "the order and beauty of the universe."[5] At the heart of this perspective is a concern, not with abstract justice, "but with the relation between creator and creature."[6] The overriding impetus for mending this relationship comes from grace and love.[7]

---

4. The point is put well by Miroslav Volf, who speaks of "*the kind of social agents capable of envisioning and creating just, truthful, and peaceful societies, and of shaping a cultural climate in which such agents will thrive*" (*Exclusion and Embrace*, 20–22, emphasis original).

5. Gunton, *Actuality of Atonement*, 90.

6. Gunton, *Actuality of Atonement*, 91.

7. Gunton, *Actuality of Atonement*, 92.

Sacrifice and Righteousness

In Isaiah 53, righteousness goes hand in hand with sacrifice. The servant's "making many righteous" occurs in immediate connection with his "bearing their iniquities [i.e., of "the many"]" (53:11).

This connection is drawn from distinct symbolic spheres in Old Testament thought: law and justice on the one hand, sacrificial ritual on the other. In their different idioms, both these concepts speak of putting wrong things right. In the poem, they are transformed by being embodied in the servant. We saw in the preceding chapter (with regard to 53:10) how the 'āšām offering functioned within Israel's sacrificial system as a means of compensation for some wrong done and as a way of reestablishing a right balance. The offering has a certain resonance with the motif of exchange, which runs throughout the poem. The servant's offering of his life for others lends itself to a sacrificial metaphor. The 'āšām itself is conceived in the Old Testament more as compensation than substitution, however, and the idea of exchange or substitution in the poem does not rest heavily on it. More important is the novelty of its application to an act of self-giving by a human being. (We will return to the idea of exchange/substitution below, in relation to the servant's humanity.)

In the life of the servant, righteousness and offering become complementary images. The question is, What does it take for God to put things right in his world? The poem's response is to emphasize both the righteousness and the self-giving of the servant. As righteousness is signified by this person's self-sacrifice, righteousness is kept from being a merely abstract thing. As self-sacrifice is signified by righteousness, it is kept from being a noble but empty gesture. The two metaphors of law and sacrifice are again brought together by the apostle Paul in the course of his argument about justification through faith in Christ (Rom. 3:21–26).

Victory

The idea of a transformed creation invokes a further metaphor from the poem's symbolic universe, namely, victory—drawn, of course, from the sphere of war. The servant will "share plunder with the strong" (53:12). This idea too is bound closely to his "pouring himself out to death," in an impossible paradox. As with the other metaphors, it does not imply a literal battlefield triumph. This point is important because such imagery is by no means foreign to the book of Isaiah; it lies behind the messianic portrait in 9:2–7 [1–6], for example. It lies too in the background narrative of the military rout of Babylon by Cyrus and in prophetic images of the desolation of that city (Isa. 13–14; 47), as well as of many others (chaps. 13–27 generally, and 36–37). Here, however, the servant's victory is woven into the composite picture of his innocence and self-sacrifice. This is a victory beyond victories, in a world in which sin and its baneful effects have not only been countered but defeated.

Resurrection

The concept of victory in the poem is bound inescapably to another notion, the survival of death. As we saw in the exegesis of 53:8–10, the poem is not absolutely clear on whether the servant died and was restored to life. Even to pose the issue in this way is slightly misleading, because the poem does not set out to furnish a biographical account of an actual historical figure. So to ask whether he died and rose again is an unanswerable question. However, the language of verses 8–10 is strongly suggestive of it, and therefore the poem points to resurrection as an element of its symbolic world. As is well known, the Old Testament's theology of resurrection is sparse. Life after death is depicted in a number of texts as a shadowy state not far removed from nonexistence, and its evocation may in some cases be no more than a rhetorical trope (e.g., Isa. 14:4–21). The specific concept of resurrection occurs in Ezekiel 37:1–14 as a metaphor for the renewal of Israel. Individual resurrection appears in Daniel 12:1–3, a text that, notably, carries an echo of Isaiah 53:11 ("making many righteous"). Isaiah knows of Death as a great enemy (28:15, 18), and 25:8 presages an eschatological swallowing up of Death forever.

While this picture is rather uneven, Jon Levenson (writing from a Jewish perspective) maintains that resurrection as a concept lies deep in the Hebrew Scriptures and Jewish tradition. The God of Israel is the God of life. The Scriptures intimate in various ways that this implies an overcoming of death. Levenson cites the miracles of Elijah and Elisha (1 Kings 17:17–24; 2 Kings 4:8–37).[8] One might add the "translations" to heaven of Elijah and Enoch (2 Kings 2:9–12; Gen. 5:24).[9] Certain psalms testify to a longing for life beyond death (e.g., 49; 73), and the notion of enduring life in the temple generates and reinforces such an expectation.[10] Levenson also cites texts that speak metaphorically of resurrection, including Ezekiel's famous valley of dry bones (Ezek. 37:1–14) and the restoration of children to

8. Levenson, *Resurrection and the Restoration of Israel*, 123.
9. The case of Enoch is somewhat ambiguous: "God took him" (Gen. 5:24). Yet the phrase is a significant deviation from the otherwise consistent refrain in the chapter: "and he died." The pseudepigraphal book of 1 Enoch is predicated on the belief that Enoch was taken to heaven.
10. Levenson, *Resurrection and the Restoration of Israel*, 98, cites Ps. 84:10–12 [11–13] and Jon. 2:3–10. He also says of Ps. 128, "It is very much to be doubted that he [the psalmist] thought the felicity of which he sang ended at the grave" (122).

the barren widow Zion (Isa. 54:1–10).[11] And he points to the LORD's words in Deuteronomy 32:39: "I kill and I make alive."[12]

In this landscape, actual revivals to life (Elijah, Elisha) are not completely separate categories from metaphorical depictions. It is difficult to drive a wedge between Ezekiel 37:1–14 and Isaiah 26:19, even though for Levenson "the dead" in 26:19 "are markedly less metaphorical than the dry bones of Ezekiel 37."[13] The relation between "literal" and "metaphorical" in this context is a kind of sliding scale. While explicit indications of individual resurrection come relatively late, they are closely related to habitual language in the Old Testament: "A full-fledged doctrine of the resurrection of the dead, when it arrives, . . . reflects certain key features of the deep structure of the theology of pre-exilic Israel."[14] All of this language is generally bound up with the existence of Israel.

Isaiah 53 thus inhabits a thought-world in which the survival of death is not a new idea. It also plays a key part in the emergence of resurrection belief specifically, because of its evident influence on Daniel 12:1–3 (in the motifs of "the wise" and "making many righteous"), along with Isaiah 25:8 and 26:19. Isaiah 53 is not unambiguously a warrant for a doctrine of individual resurrection, since the conceptual background we have noted is frequently oriented toward the survival of Israel. Yet, by the same token, it cannot be ruled out. The topic is related to the question of whether the servant in Isaiah 53 is an individual or corporate Israel, which (as we noted earlier) cannot be finally resolved. Most importantly, resurrection is not presented here as simply a belief in the afterlife, but

---

11. Levenson, *Resurrection and the Restoration of Israel*, 145–46. On the theme of children restored (142–44), he cites Isa. 43:1–8; 44:1–5; 48:7–19.

12. Levenson, *Resurrection and the Restoration of Israel*, 180.

13. Levenson, *Resurrection and the Restoration of Israel*, 200.

14. Levenson, *Resurrection and the Restoration of Israel*, 180.

rather as the outcome of the servant's life of righteousness and self-offering.

▦ Isaiah 53 in the New Testament

We have been trying to understand Isaiah 53 on its own terms and in its own conceptual world. While we have attempted to come as close as possible to its meaning in itself, we have been aware that it is in many ways open to fresh interpretations. We began to observe in chapter 1 that the poem has a depth and variety that has touched readers in diverse ways, depending on their situations and their capacity for sensitive understanding. It is indeed a gift to the believing communities who have received it, a gift whose genius is to stimulate profound reflection on the ways of God in the world, and to do so in an ever-renewing fashion.

The book of Isaiah itself, as one of the poem's most important contexts, gives its own first response to it in an exhortation to Zion (personified as a woman) to sing, to burst into song, and to shout because a time of joy after sorrow has dawned for her (54:1). In this way, the tribute to the Suffering Servant is bound into the book's larger story of the LORD's salvation of his people. The latter chapters of the book contain pointers to the ways in which this might be so. The Suffering Servant becomes a model for "servants" (54:17), and those who are worthy of the name become a critical presence in the community redeemed from exile (63:15–19; 65:13–16). The redemption of Zion after exile is an unfinished business, and so too is the work of the servant.

Other biblical books and versions selected their own highlights and angles. We have noted hints of messianic interpretation in the Qumran Isaiah Scroll and in Zechariah 12:10, an emphasis on the glorification of the servant in LXX, and a wisdom orientation in Wisdom of Solomon, with its interest in the ultimate fate of the righteous in contrast to the wicked, even after death.

I want now to consider some of the ways in which the poem has made an impact on those who have received it, and still continues to do so. It is not possible to offer an extensive account here; fuller accounts of the reception of Isaiah 53 are on offer elsewhere.[15] My aim is more modest: to show the poem's potential for opening up avenues of perception in the minds of those who read and meditate on it. The variety of its reception is partly attributable to the tensions within it, particularly the tension between the servant's humiliation and exaltation, or suffering and triumph. As Martin Hengel has shown, these opposite poles have been differently calibrated in various writings after the Old Testament period.[16] The motif of vicarious suffering is not consistently taken up, for example, and appears to be less prominent in texts that lean toward collective interpretations of the servant.[17] Hengel also finds a tension between vicarious suffering and triumphant judgment, the former present in LXX (albeit weakened in comparison with MT), but the latter predominating in Wisdom 5.[18] He concludes, "Basically, we can say that wherever the motif of the judge is prominent, the motif of vicarious suffering disappears."[19]

In principle, variety of emphasis and interpretation is also true of New Testament receptions of Isaiah 53. It should be

15. E.g., Janowski and Stuhlmacher, *Suffering Servant*; Bellinger and Farmer, *Jesus and the Suffering Servant*; Witherington, *Isaiah Old and New*.

16. Hengel and Bailey, "Effective History of Isaiah 53," 89.

17. Hengel and Bailey, "Effective History of Isaiah 53," 98–101. The term "vicarious" is defined as above (chap. 3): "[suffering] in place of and for the benefit of others."

18. Hengel and Bailey, "Effective History of Isaiah 53," 123–24.

19. Hengel and Bailey, "Effective History of Isaiah 53," 146.

said that the extent of the poem's influence on the New Testament writers is hard to measure with any certainty. A number of passages allude expressly to it, as in Matthew 8:17, where we read, "This was to fulfill what was spoken through the prophet Isaiah." Morna Hooker identifies eight such unambiguous allusions, of which seven have introductory formulae such as "It is written" to show they are quotations.[20] The issue is less clear in cases where the text seems to reflect some aspect of the poem, but where no quotation is signaled. In such instances (e.g., Rom. 4:25; Phil. 2:6–11), there may be influence from other Old Testament texts, either instead of Isaiah 53 or alongside it. Even where an allusion to the poem is explicit, there can also be a question about what the writer understands by it. For example, in Acts 8:32–33, which makes no reference to the servant's suffering for others' sins, should we suppose that Luke intends to call to mind the whole context of Isaiah 53:7, together with that theme, or, conversely, that he has deliberately passed over it?[21] In such cases, we cannot be sure of all that was in the author's mind. We have only the text itself and have to interpret it contextually and exegetically according to what seems to make the best sense of it. The same must be said about how far Jesus may have understood himself and his ministry in the light of the servant-poem (the question that Hooker was principally addressing). Again, we have to be content with the picture presented to us in the Gospels.[22]

---

20. Hooker, "Did the Use of Isaiah 53 to Interpret His Mission Begin with Jesus?," 90. The eight are Matt. 8:17; Mark 15:28; Luke 22:37; John 12:38; Acts 8:32–33; Rom. 10:16; 15:21; 1 Pet. 2:22–25 (Hooker, 90–93). Of these, Mark 15:28 is widely thought to be a late addition to Mark and is consigned to a footnote in NRSV.

21. Hooker thinks Acts 8 stops short just at the point where it is about to move to interpretation and therefore functions only as a prooftext ("Did the Use of Isaiah 53 to Interpret His Mission Begin with Jesus?," 91–92).

22. A quite different approach to the influence of Isa. 53 on both Jesus and the New Testament writers is taken by Otto Betz in the same volume as Hooker's essay. Betz refers to a long scholarly debate on the point, with H. W. Wolff on one side, arguing

Our interest here is in what sort of use New Testament texts make of the poem. Not all of them highlight the idea of exchange or substitution. Several, however, do take up the idea that the servant suffered somehow "for us" or in our place. Jesus in Mark 10:45 declares that he has come to "give his life as a ransom for many" (*anti pollōn*), recalling the exchange motif in Isaiah 53:4–6 and also drawing together elements in 53:12 ("poured out his life to death," "bore the sin of many").

These New Testament appropriations of substitution have their own contexts and aims. To take one important example, 1 Peter 2:22–25 cites Isaiah 53:5b ("by his wounds you have been healed") in one of the New Testament's most carefully elaborated expressions of Christ's atoning death. The author has drawn in several elements of Isaiah 53 around this key text. He cites Isaiah 53:9b verbatim to express Christ's innocence as the necessary premise of all that follows (1 Pet. 2:22).[23] He then reworks elements in Isaiah 53:5 with his proclamation that Christ "himself has borne our sins" (*hos tas hamartias hēmōn autos anēnenken*)[24] and that "you" have been "healed by his wounds" (*tō mōlōpi iathēte*), all within his portrayal of Christ's atoning death on the cross (1 Pet. 2:24). The intention of Christ's death ("that we might die to sin and live to righteousness") has echoes of Isaiah 53:11b. The intervening verse, 1 Peter 2:23, recalls the servant's unresisting silence (Isa. 53:7). Finally, in 1 Peter 2:25, the sinners who are saved by Christ's death had once "strayed like sheep," in the metaphor of Isaiah 53:6a. The author of 1 Peter, therefore, has thoughtfully applied the description of the Suffering Servant to his argument about

---

that the poem would have been well known to Jesus and the early Christians, and R. Bultmann in contrast taking a more skeptical view. Betz favors the view of Wolff and is critical of Hooker's method ("Jesus and Isaiah 53," esp. 70–74).

23. The citation varies slightly from LXX; 1 Pet. 2:22 has *hamartian* whereas LXX has *anomian*.

24. LXX has *etraumatisthē dia tas anomias hēmōn*, "he was bruised for our sins."

the atoning and sanctifying death of Christ. But it is important to pay attention to the context. The author's immediate concern is the suffering of the people to whom he is writing. His appeal is to suffer patiently, which draws on Christ's own patient suffering as an example, even though Christ was innocent (1 Pet. 2:21–22). The vicarious nature of Christ's death (vv. 24–25) is drawn into the author's encouragement to endure. There is no express mention of resurrection in this text (though of course it is a premise of the whole letter; see 1 Pet. 1:3–5).

Likewise, the apostle Paul's interpretation of Isaiah 53:5 in Romans 4:24–25 rests on his contention that Christ's death had the purpose of dealing with "our" sins. Paul's argument too is based on a reading of Isaiah 53 as a whole. Here, however, Christ's dying "for our sins" and his rising "for our justification" are combined into a single nexus.[25]

As we have noted above, the New Testament appropriation of Isaiah 53 is by no means confined to the motif of the servant's sacrifice in exchange for the punishment due for human sin. Matthew provides the leading example (Matt. 8:17), when he treats Jesus's healings as a fulfillment of Isaiah 53:4. To pursue this point further, I want to look more closely at two other New Testament receptions of the Isaianic poem: the motif of the servant's glorification in John's Gospel, and the servant's humiliation and exaltation in Philippians 2:6–11.

The influence of the Isaianic poem on John's Gospel may be seen in three passages that employ the motif of "lifting up" on the basis of Isaiah 52:13 LXX. In John, the "lifting up" of Christ is applied to his literal lifting up on the cross, but with the additional implication of his exaltation through his resurrection and ascension. The Gospel exploits the potential ambiguity

---

25. For remarks on Paul's appropriation of "righteousness" in Rom. 5:19, see comments above on Isa. 53:11, in chap. 3.

in the verb *hupsoō* ("lift up") in order to express the paradox of exaltation through humiliation that is present in Isaiah 53, applying it to Christ's death, resurrection, and ascension. Catrin Williams traces a certain progression in three Johannine texts that focus on this theme. In John 3:14, with its allusion to the Mosaic raising of the serpent image in the wilderness (Num. 21:4–9), the accent is on the literal raising of Jesus on the cross. John 8:28–29, where the lifting up is associated with the telling phrase "I am he," intimating the close relationship between Jesus and the Father (cf. Isa. 43:10 LXX), is more open to connotations of Christ's return to his Father in heaven. But the motif is developed most fully in John 12:27–40. In this text, Christ is said to have been "lifted up from the earth" (12:32), implying that his exaltation goes beyond the cross to include his resurrection and ascension. The use of Isaiah 53 to express the full meaning of this sequence of events extends to the phrase "[I] will draw all people [*pantas*] to myself," echoing the "many" in Isaiah 53:11–12. The appropriation of Isaiah 53 is also evident in the motif of "seeing." This connection is adumbrated in John 12:35–36a, with its use of the "light" motif, employed in Isaiah as a metaphor for salvation and now applied to Christ himself (cf. John 8:12). In verses 36b–40, the "seeing" motif is explicitly related to Isaiah 53:1. Even deeper in the background lies Isaiah 6:9–10.[26]

It emerges from these observations that John has reflected profoundly on Isaiah 53, finding in it the close association of God and the servant, the juxtaposition of "lifting up" and glorification, and the motif of "seeing" as a function of spiritual insight. (Note the pairing of seeing and understanding in 52:15, following 6:9–10, and the development of this motif in 53:10–11.) In John, the cross of Christ is presented "as a

---

26. Williams, "Another Look at 'Lifting Up' in the Gospel of John," 63–68.

means to divine revelation and salvation for those with eyes to 'see.'"[27] Williams concludes that the lifting up of Christ in John embraces the entire nexus from cross to resurrection.[28]

The case of John illustrates the creativity and imagination that the first Christians brought to their reading of the Scriptures as they sought to understand the full meaning of Jesus's life, death, and resurrection. Possibilities latent in Isaiah 53 were selected and reconfigured both to explore and express their nascent apprehension of Christ.

A further example is afforded by Philippians 2:6–11. This famous passage, often called a hymn, may have had its place in the life of the church before Paul adopted it when he wrote Philippians. While it does not explicitly cite Isaiah 53, its thematic echoes of the Isaianic poem have often been noted.[29] Here is one who "emptied himself," was born a human, took the form of a slave (or servant), was humbled, and submitted to death. Yet, astonishingly, he was then exalted to a place of highest honor "to the glory of God the Father." The confession in Philippians 2:10–11, that at Jesus's name every knee should bend and every tongue confess, clearly alludes to Isaiah 45:23 and expresses the belief that in Christ the one true God ultimately triumphs over every rival power. The hymn comes close to the language of Isaiah 53 at several points. Christ's self-emptying (Phil. 2:7) echoes the servant's "pouring himself out" to death (Isa. 53:12). The twice-repeated term "form" (*morphē*, Phil. 2:6–7) resonates with the servant's marred appearance in Isaiah 52:12 and that "he had no beauty or noble aspect" (53:2; NRSV: "no form or

---

27. Williams, "Another Look at 'Lifting Up' in the Gospel of John," 68.

28. Williams, "Another Look at 'Lifting Up' in the Gospel of John," 68–70. For support she cites Lincoln, *Gospel according to Saint John*, 13.

29. E.g., N. T. Wright, *Paul and the Faithfulness of God*, 680–90. Wright takes all of Isa. 40–55 as background to the text. YHWH's triumphant return to Zion is realized through the Suffering Servant. In the servant Jesus, the one God defeats all his enemies.

majesty"). Christ's obedience to the point of death (Phil. 2:8) recalls the servant's acquiescence "like a lamb brought to the slaughter" (Isa. 53:7), melded with the phrase "poured out his life to death" (53:12). As the servant would be highly exalted (Isa. 52:13), so now God highly exalts Christ (Phil. 2:9).

The Philippians hymn is no mere repetition of the Isaiah poem, nor is it influenced exclusively by it. Philippians' allusion to Isaiah 45:23, for example, suggests that the hymn knows the overarching sweep of Isaiah 40–55. And its use of *morphē*, "form," does not come from the LXX translation of the poem but is the hymn's own device to produce an ironic contrast between "form of God" and "form of a slave/servant." It is possible, too, to find other typologies behind the hymn, such as the figure of Adam, who may be said to have snatched at equality with God.[30]

Yet these other connections do not diminish the hymn's evident reflection on the servant-poem. The important point about that reflection is the hymn's creative freedom in using it for its own theological purposes. Strikingly, there is nothing in the hymn of the theme of exchange, which is prominent in the Isaianic poem and taken up by other New Testament writers. Rather, the hymn chooses to highlight the servant's trajectory from humiliation to exaltation. In its application to Christ, this now entails an initial descent. Christ does not merely "pour out his life" but "empties himself" of the legitimate claim he possessed to the status of God. And at the nadir, where he becomes "obedient to the point of death," there comes the decisive gloss "even death on a cross" (Phil. 2:8). The desperate picture of the abject human being in the Isaiah poem is now given a new shape in the unparalleled pain and humiliation of an instrument of torture designed for that very purpose.

30. N. T. Wright, *Paul and the Faithfulness of God*, 686.

Paul's hymn is a vivid example of reading an Old Testament text through the lens of the Christ-event, yet not so as merely to subsume it, but rather to draw on its imaginative power in order to interpret the overwhelming experience of the death and resurrection of Christ.

Finally, "taking the form of a servant" is applied to the life of Christ's followers in the church: "Let the same mind be in you that was in Christ Jesus" (Phil. 2:5 NRSV). The hymn extolling Christ's humiliation-to-exaltation is introduced in the context of an exhortation to Christian disciples to practice the virtues that Christ taught them (vv. 1–4). Just as the servant in Isaiah formed "servants" by his willing humiliation (Isa. 54:17), so disciples are exhorted to make humility the keynote of their relationships together. This is not mere ethical instruction but an outflow of their participation in Christ. The shape of Christ's life, death, resurrection, and ascension is to be the shape of the life of the church.

What emerges from these illustrations of the New Testament's use of Isaiah 53 is how the writers have taken up aspects of the poem in pursuit of their particular arguments. They do no violence to it, since the themes are present in the poem. They do demonstrate the suggestive power of the poem and how it can be applied faithfully to particular contextual needs and purposes.

The Servant's Humanity

I want now to shift the lens slightly, as we come to consider the servant's humanity. In doing so, I want to consider it, not so much as a matter of New Testament reception, but more directly in relation to its Christian reception, and with a view to its significance for the humanity of Christ.

We have spent some time considering the servant's human agency in relation to the Lord's. The relationship between God and humanity is one of the running motifs of the Old Testament, beginning with humanity as being in the "image of God" (Gen. 1:26) and moving through successive versions of covenant (chiefly the Abrahamic, Mosaic, and Davidic). The servant plays into this story of the human relationship to God in creation and covenant. In considering the servant's humanity more closely, therefore, we aim to do justice to the poem itself and also to recognize the importance of the real humanity of Jesus, which lies at the heart of Christian belief. Early Christians had to contend for this conviction against powerful opposition from Gnostics, who thought that Christ's divinity would have been compromised by taking on actual human flesh. Such a view could only survive as long as it did by deliberately looking away from the Old Testament. Isaiah 53 depicts, before all else, a profoundly human experience.

It is certainly not alone in doing so. We have noticed a number of similarities between the servant's experience and that of other Old Testament figures. The book of Job is a paradigmatic account of an innocent sufferer, with his excruciating wish for nonexistence in Job 3 and his sustained pursuit of God out of the injustice of his pain. Jeremiah, like the Isaianic servant, was "like a lamb led to the slaughter" (Jer. 11:19). The casual or callous enmity of others, even of former friends, is a leading motif of the Psalms. The poet in Psalm 25 complains that he is "lonely and afflicted" (25:16), in terms reminiscent of Isaiah 53:3–4, 7.[31] The Psalms' darkest picture of isolation and abandonment is in Psalm 88, with its terrible finale in verse 18 [19]: "You have caused friend and neighbor to shun me; my

---

31. The phrase in Ps. 25:16 is *yāḥid wəʿānî*; *ʿānî* is related to words in Isa. 53:4 (*ûməʿunneh*) and 53:7 (*naʿāneh*).

companions are in darkness" (NRSV). A plural voice in Psalm 44 protests in vivid language that the Lord himself has "broken us . . . and covered us with deep darkness" (44:19 [20]), that they have been "killed all day long, and accounted as sheep for the slaughter" (v. 22 [23] NRSV), and that they are innocent (vv. 17–18 [18–19], 20–21 [21–22]). The book of Lamentations is dedicated, in deeply emotive language, to the graphic depiction of unbearable pain, sometimes with a sense of excess, beyond any deserving (e.g., Lam. 2:18–22).

Does the suffering of the servant add anything new to such depictions of human misery? There is, perhaps, no measure for the intensity of suffering. But Isaiah 53 has something vitally important that these other accounts lack: the servant's resolute silence. The contrast between this silence and the many voices of lament in the Old Testament is conspicuous and hardly accidental. It would be an intriguing intertextual study to consider which of the many expressions of anguish in Psalms, Job, and Lamentations the Isaianic servant might reasonably have taken on his lips. A lead might be found in the book of Isaiah itself, with the complaint of Jacob-Israel in 40:27 ("My way is hidden from the Lord, and my right is disregarded by my God," NRSV). In this way, the fate of the servant in Isaiah 53 would be bound into the story of servant-Israel in chapters 40–55 and Israel's sense of having been abandoned by the Lord in the destruction of Jerusalem and the Babylonian exile. Yet to follow this tack would be to miss the point. For one thing, the reader's curiosity may arise from an interest in "what really happened" to the servant, which, as we have seen, is impossible to answer. But more important, there is something self-contained about Isaiah 53, and it is part of its poetic art that the servant is allowed no speech.

How should we evaluate this aspect of the poem? Does the poem imply that silence in the face of suffering is somehow more commendable than giving voice to anguish? However, the balance of the Old Testament witness stands against this. We might focus the question further by bringing it to bear on the demeanor of Jesus in his last days.

The warrant for doing so lies in the New Testament's hermeneutical practice of interpreting Jesus in the light of the Old Testament Scriptures, as we have already illustrated across a range of New Testament writers. According to Luke, Jesus himself gave a decisive lead to this practice in his conversation with the two disciples on the Emmaus road (Luke 24). Such New Testament precedents have been taken by modern interpreters as a mandate for further canonical reflection.[32] For example, David Ford has pondered the relation between the sufferings of Job and those of Jesus. He regards the book of Job as unsurpassed in its capacity to convey and address the deepest human anguish. Then, concerning Job and Jesus, he writes,

> Job, read and reread alongside the Gospel, offers a discipline that might train our attention to concentrate on the cries of Jesus and, through him, on the cries he hears now. Job helps to draw attention back again and again to the intractable, unassimilable and unconceptualisable quality of intense suffering as expressed in the cry from the cross.[33]

In contemplating Jesus's passion, one might think of his torment in the garden of Gethsemane, when he prays, "Father, if you are willing, remove this cup from me," and is so physically and emotionally overcome that he seems to sweat blood (Luke 22:42–44 NRSV). The episode foreshadows the cross. But Ford centers his attention on the cross itself and especially Jesus's cries from it, which for Ford are the culmination of a life of

32. For a defense of this in principle, see Ford, *Christian Wisdom*, 168–69.
33. Ford, *Christian Wisdom*, 170–71.

crying out and are aligned with the Old Testament's wisdom and prophetic traditions.[34] In his agony, Jesus cries, "My God, my God, why have you forsaken me?" (Mark 15:34 NRSV), which echoes the first line of the great lament in Psalm 22. At the point of death, Jesus cries out in a loud voice, "Father, into your hands I commend my spirit" (Luke 23:46 NRSV).

When we try to understand Jesus's suffering, the role of speech is indispensable: both his own words recorded in the Gospels, and not just on the cross but throughout his ministry; and also the rich seams of Old Testament wisdom, psalmody, and prophecy, as exemplified by Ford's use of Job as testimony to the unfathomable depths of human pain. Yet there is a paradox in the role of speech in suffering, for words ultimately cannot express the fullness of those depths. In the passage quoted above, Ford points effectively—through language that almost breaks down under the strain—to this inexpressibility.

Isaiah 53 knows this reality well and testifies to it from another angle. The servant's silence is one of the poem's most powerful effects. It is no accidental omission of speech, but rather the presentation of a mute witness, which is as powerful as speech, to untold pain. As readers, we may itch to know more of what may have lain behind this haunting portrait. Yet there are also things into which we cannot bear to look. The poem itself flinches from realistic depiction. The servant was "one from whom one looks away" (v. 3). That natural reaction, confessed by people who had come to see his truth, is a caution to the reader. Which of us can focus intently on the deepest anguish? It is natural to "look away," to protect ourselves from the horror of the full potential for human grief. Yet it is precisely

---

34. He writes, "[*Jesus's*] *wisdom is shaped through the passionate multiple intensities embodied in all the cries that have pervaded his ministry and which climax now in his passion and death*" (Ford, *Christian Wisdom*, 33, emphasis original).

this paradox into which the poem draws us: to imagine the most profound, unmitigated pain.

The portrait of the servant is completely human. It is human distress experienced by the one and contemplated tremulously by others, ourselves, "the many," who are disturbed by it because we too are human. The same can be said about our contemplation of the passion and death of Jesus.[35] The Gospel accounts differ from Isaiah 53 in their vivid, albeit restrained, depictions of his last days. We imagine the pain of the scourging and the crown of thorns; the backbreaking weight of the cross, borne while he was already terribly weakened by torture, heat, and thirst; the unspeakable agony of rough, heavy nails driven through hands and feet; and all of it magnified by the brutally routine raising of a cross and cruel, unending hours in the sun.

And yet here our imagination also fails. The agony is finally unspeakable. In the end, there is a silence in it that we cannot penetrate.

The Gospel writers, in different ways, also notice the actual silences of Jesus in his last days. Luke reports that, when questioned by Herod, to whom he had been sent by Pilate, "Jesus gave him no answer" (Luke 23:9 NRSV). The motif of Jesus's silence is most conspicuous in Matthew, which records almost no words of Jesus during his passion. His last words in ordinary speech come during his arrest, when he is concerned to show that what is happening to him is in fulfillment of prophecy (Matt. 26:47–56). Interrogated shortly afterward by the high priest, "Jesus was silent" (26:63a). When Pilate invites him to respond to the charges made against him, "[Jesus] gave him no answer, not even to a single charge, so that the governor was greatly amazed" (27:14 NRSV). Twice he merely turns back

---

35. Sonderegger also notes a connection between Jesus's silence and Isa. 53 (*Systematic Theology*, 1:232).

accusations with "You have said so" (26:64; 27:11b; though in the former he adds a prophecy-fulfillment statement about the Son of Man). Jesus's final words in Matthew (and Mark), in contrast to Luke and John, are the cry of dereliction (Matt. 27:46; cf. Mark 15:33–39; Luke 23:32–49; John 19:26–30).[36] For Matthew, it looks very much as if Jesus's silence during his passion is one more fulfillment of prophecy, in this case Isaiah 53:7.[37]

The exploration of Jesus's silence does not end there. For all his irreducible humanity, there is another decisive factor: that "in Christ God was reconciling the world to himself" (2 Cor. 5:19 NRSV). The servant "bore the sin of many" (Isa. 53:12). Did he know he was doing this? Did it play any part in his self-abandonment or his endurance? Could he even grasp the meaning of something so novel in the history of human tragedy? These unanswerable questions become even more acute in the case of Jesus. The Gospels tell us that he not only went unresisting to his awful death but that he was burdened with the sense that this was his destiny (most tellingly, in John 18:11). And as for what he went through in order to bear the sin of the world, this lies far beyond the reach of sinful human beings to comprehend. As Fleming Rutledge puts it, speaking of the cry of dereliction ("My God, my God, why have you forsaken me?"), "We cannot plumb the depths of this cry—more like a shriek or abysmal groan—for truly it comes as Christ descends into the hell from which he delivers us."[38]

What does this inscrutable silence at the heart of the crucifixion teach us about how we might rightly regard it? It has

36. I am grateful to Andrew (A. T.) Lincoln for pointing this out to me, especially the pattern in Matthew, in a private communication.

37. Lincoln also suggests that Matthew might in addition have had Isa. 53:8 in mind: "By a corruption of justice he was taken off."

38. Rutledge, *Crucifixion*, 533.

inspired more visual representation than any other single event in human history. Some medieval art tended to be stylized, avoiding any hint of realism. Other depictions have veered toward the realistic. The most striking in recent times was perhaps Mel Gibson's film *The Passion of the Christ* (2004). Gibson wanted us to look the horror of the passion squarely in the face, as those who loved and followed Jesus found themselves compelled to do. Realism itself is inevitably limited, however, because no amount of close-up inspection of physical torment can disclose the true depth of Christ's suffering, a depth that was uniquely his because he was the Christ. Differently, Matthias Grünewald's Isenheim Altarpiece (ca. 1510–15), with its depiction of the horror of the cross, incorporated both the realistic and the figural. The image represents, at one and the same time, both what is present to the viewer and what can be seen only by revelation. On one side of the cross, mourners display their grief at the death of the human Jesus. On the other side, John the Baptist, curiously detached and with a sacrificial lamb, points to Christ, indicating that the human reality veils a divine reality giving it its true meaning.

Yet the tradition of visual representation also trades on silence and invites the viewer's silent contemplation in turn.

One telling example of this contemplation of human suffering is in a kind of depiction of Christ that became known as the "man of sorrows," taking a cue from Isaiah 53:3. This style of depiction, as described by John Sawyer, focuses on human pain itself, without a spatial or temporal context and with few pointers to theological meaning. Rather, the anguish of the "man of sorrows" enables the viewer's identification with the sufferer. The influence of Isaiah 53 on "man of sorrows" images is nowhere explicit but widely assumed. One striking correspondence between the Isaiah poem and this artistic style is the absence of context: like the "man of sorrows," the servant in Isaiah 53 is unnamed and furnished with no historical, contextual, or biographical information. Both the poem and the visual image provide stark confrontations with the human potential for profound, inexpressible pain. Sawyer takes the point further: "The open-endedness of Isaiah 53, like the lack of spatial and temporal detail in the 'Man of Sorrows' image, makes it an ideal expression of the belief that Christ's suffering incorporates the suffering of all humanity."[39] This thought finds surprising but eloquent support in the work of Oscar Wilde, who wrote with deep poignancy of the suffering of his fellow inmates and himself during his two-year imprisonment under homosexuality laws that prevailed in England in the 1890s. The systematic terror and dehumanization of people, under the shadow of another's lonely execution, is portrayed with great pathos in *The Ballad of Reading Gaol*. The picture of desperate isolation is stark:

> And never a human voice comes near
>   To speak a gentle word:
> And the eye that watches through the door
>   Is pitiless and hard:
> And by all forgot, we rot and rot,
>   With soul and body marred.[40]

The solidarity in suffering is interwoven with the symbolism of the passion of Christ, who died for all. The connection between

39. Sawyer, *Fifth Gospel*, 93. In his account, instances of the genre are found in works by Bellini, Mantegna, and Dürer, and its influence is seen too in Titian, Rubens, and Rembrandt (92–93). In support of his thesis, Sawyer extensively cites G. Schiller, *Iconography of Christian Art*. Sawyer also documents medieval depictions of details from Isa. 53 that are applied, often gruesomely, to moments in Christ's passion, for example, his being "led" to his death (89–90), the "shearing" of the Lamb of God, and his "bearing" of our sins, in which Christ is depicted as weighed down by the burden of them (90–91).

40. Wilde, *De Profundis/The Ballad of Reading Gaol*, 137.

the "man of sorrows" and the common suffering of humanity
is elaborated in Wilde's other prison work, *De Profundis*, an
extended letter to his former lover, Lord Alfred Douglas. There
is nothing in all literature to compare, he says, with the human
tragedy of Christ's passion, culminating in the crucifixion, "the
coronation-ceremony of Sorrow."[41] In his description of Christ
as bearing the burden of all human sin and suffering, Wilde
gives imaginative play to its endless scope:

> There is still something to me almost incredible in the idea of a young
> Galilean peasant imagining that he could bear on his own shoulders
> the burden of the entire world: all that had been already done and
> suffered, and all that was yet to be done and suffered: the sins of Nero,
> of Caesar Borgia, of Alexander VI, and of him who was Emperor of
> Rome and Priest of the Sun: the sufferings of those whose name is
> Legion and whose dwelling is among the tombs, oppressed nation-
> alities, factory children, thieves, people in prison, outcasts, those
> who are dumb under oppression and whose silence is heard only of
> God.[42]

The passage of nearly a century and a half after Wilde's imprisonment has added unspeakably to history's repertoire of
grief. But his twice-repeated admonition to his friend makes
his central point: "Whatever happens to another happens to
oneself."[43]

Aloneness and Substitution

The servant was radically alone, forsaken by all. The narrative underlying Isaiah 53 does not disclose whether the "we"
speakers in verses 1–6 changed their view of the servant in time

41. Wilde, *De Profundis/The Ballad of Reading Gaol*, 71.
42. Wilde, *De Profundis/The Ballad of Reading Gaol*, 70–71.
43. Wilde, *De Profundis/The Ballad of Reading Gaol*, 70.

to offer him companionship and consolation. That is another silence. Jesus too was finally alone with his burden of salvation. "Could you not stay awake with me one hour?" he remonstrated with his sleepy friends in Gethsemane (Matt. 26:40 NRSV). "I do not know the man!" protested fearful Peter in the high priest's house (26:72). The friends faltered in their resolve to stay with him. Yet his mission was such that no one could have accompanied him to the end of it. Loneliness and abandonment came with the territory.

And this was entailed in the "exchange." It is a running motif in the Isaiah poem that the servant acted in the place of others. He was innocent, but he paid the price of their guilt. He was battered to the point of death so that they would not suffer the consequences of their own sins. "He was wounded because of [or for] our rebelliousness." The pattern of exchange is imprinted on the form of 53:4–5. In our attempt to understand this, we used the concept of "vicarious" suffering, in which one person suffers, in some sense, on behalf of others.

The poem does not spell out what is meant by the exchange. The notion of exchange is seminal, and it raised questions for others to pursue, both in and beyond the New Testament. We noticed above, and in the preceding chapter (especially on Isa. 53:5, 11), how it was taken up by the New Testament writers. Christ died for sinners so that they might live and in order to make them righteous. The poem's "many" is translated into all humanity. The glorification of the servant through suffering becomes the glorification of Christ through his "lifting up" on the cross so that he might draw "all people" to himself (John 12:32). The New Testament therefore adds new layers of meaning to the poem's framework. Even so, questions remain.

What is involved in "for us"? What might it mean to say that Jesus died "in our place"? One distinction commonly made is between "substitution" and "representation." Is Jesus our substitute or our representative? No such terms will apply perfectly in this case, not least because they may be capable of a range of meanings. However, there is merit in affirming both as a means of thinking about the "exchange" effected in Christ's atonement. As representative, Jesus can stand in relation to all people in all times and places—the ultimate extension of Isaiah 53's "many." It is as if they are deemed to be present because he is present. This is somewhat like the idea that elected members of a political assembly represent their constituents, or conference delegates their institutions. They may stand with or alongside those they represent and share in their situation. But they do not act instead of them. A substitute, however, may actually take my place. For Colin Gunton, the "representative" idea cannot cope with the underlying issue in the atonement, which is a state of war in the unredeemed creation. Therefore, "we have to say that Jesus is our substitute, because he does for us what we cannot do for ourselves."[44] Representation and substitution are not necessarily at odds with each other, however. When they are taken together, Christ may be said to have stood in the place of all humanity in order to reconcile all humanity to God. Most importantly, substitution is "not a legal transaction, but an act of unmerited grace."[45]

Entailed in Jesus's substitution for sinful humanity is his abandonment by both God and people. His abandonment is

44. Gunton, *Actuality of Atonement*, 164–65. I am grateful to Dee Carter for pointing me to Gunton's work on this topic. Using different terminology, Geyser-Fouché and Munengwa speak of Christ's "place-taking" as both "inclusive" and "exclusive," corresponding respectively to the concepts of representation and substitution, as used above ("Concept of Vicarious Suffering," 5).

45. Gunton, *Actuality of Atonement*, 92. Behind this statement lies a critique of the idea of substitution as *penal*. The understanding of atonement within legal categories may be traced to Anselm, but, as Rutledge too has argued, this is a misunderstanding of Anselm. The concept of substitution as penal comes in only later (Rutledge, *Crucifixion*, 165–66).

expressed most directly in that heartrending cry of dereliction ("My God, my God, why have you forsaken me?"). But it is also symbolized by Jesus's silences, themselves an echo and a fulfillment of the silence of the servant. The one who bore the burden of the "many" necessarily bore it alone. Otherwise there could be no exchange, no substitution.[46]

---

46. Rutledge sees in the cry of dereliction an expression of unfathomable pain and finds a deep connection between that cry and the substitution of Jesus for sinful humanity (*Crucifixion*, 530–33). She argues strongly against the idea of *penal* substitution but finds the substitutionary nature of Christ's death inescapable, as a complement to a *Christus Victor* interpretation, in which Christ conquers the powers of evil.

5

The Servant in the Church's Ministry

Our interest in the great portrait of the servant in Isaiah 53 has been, from the outset, a Christian one. In what ways does the servant speak of Christ? My aim in the intervening chapters has been to offer some answers to that question. It will be clear that this is not a straightforward matter. It is mistaken to suppose that Isaiah 53 steps aside from its immediate context in the Babylonian period in order simply to disclose a person and events that lie, from its perspective, in the far future.

The poem, rather, had a journey. This emerged in our close study of the text (chap. 3), in which we noticed the early stages of its reception by means of comparisons between the standard Hebrew text and other ancient versions, especially the Great Isaiah Scroll (1QIsaᵃ) and the Greek translation of the Bible (LXX). We went on to consider ways in which a whole range of readers had been influenced by the poem, and we saw that it was possible for their interpretations to show great variations while being in their own way valid responses to the text before them. This was as true of the New Testament readings as it was of other ancient literature, and indeed of postbiblical art. In these final pages, I want to ask how we may respond to what we have seen. We will start with the hermeneutical question and then go on to say something about approaching the text in preaching, ministry, and reflection.

Interpreting the Servant as Christ

I have painted a picture of the interpretation of Isaiah 53 as being rather like a stream running through history, with interpreters finding that aspects of the poem spoke sharply to their own concerns. For the New Testament writers, the poem spoke of Christ's life, death, and resurrection. In what way can we think that their conviction was true?

The question has traditionally been answered by reference to concepts like typology. In typology, the interpreter recognizes resemblances between the first discernible meanings of a text and later ones that it comes to take on. Thus Joshua bringing salvation to Israel by taking the land of Canaan becomes a type of Jesus bringing salvation to the world by overcoming the enemies of God on the cross. The two are connected by the shared idea of God bringing salvation. When this concept is applied to Isaiah 53, it can deal with the fact that the poem was first understood in the era of the Babylonian exile, and either was occasioned by the actual experience of an individual (unknown to us) or was a sophisticated reflection on the meaning of the suffering of the people of Israel—or perhaps both of these. When the poem was later adopted as a way of understanding Christ, this depended on discerning fundamental similarities between his life, death, and resurrection and those older, seminal meanings. The same applies in principle to other receptions of the poem along the way, such as its application to the resurrection of the martyred faithful in Daniel 12.

For this to work, typology cannot merely be a technique, however effective. Behind it lies a question of truth. Why should we think particular typological interpretations are true? The answer depends on the belief that the Scriptures speak truly of the one God who was made known in Israel and, in due course, in Christ. If there is a convincing relationship between the Suffering Servant of Isaiah 53 and Jesus Christ, it lies in the unity of the divine being and purpose and in God's presence in and through historical events and persons. The poem expresses things that are true about God and human beings, and for this reason can echo and re-echo wherever and whenever these great themes are in play. Reapplications of old texts are always open to the criticism that they have been read wrongly or poorly. It is the interpreter's responsibility to decide whether readings convincingly illuminate both the text and the reality to which they would apply it.

The point should be further qualified. It is not just that there are resemblances between the former and the latter persons and events, but rather that they are all together part of a single story. There is an organic unity. The book of Isaiah as a whole testifies to this. Its underlying narrative of Zion builds on the concept of the LORD's election of Jerusalem as Israel's capital city, in which God installed his chosen king, David, as his "son" (Pss. 2; 132; 2 Sam. 7). While the significance of historical Jerusalem is never lost, Isaiah develops the idea of glorified Zion as the place where the LORD's faithful people dwell as a beacon of his *torah* to all nations (Isa. 2:2–4). Finally, Zion, the "mountain of the LORD," takes on eschatological overtones when it becomes the place where the LORD will prepare a feast for all peoples, remove "the veil" that is spread over them, and swallow up death forever (25:6–8). In a similar way, Isaiah 40–48 uses the trope of "former and latter things" to express both continuity in the story of the LORD with his people and the emergence out of it of things entirely new. Indeed, the LORD himself is both "the first" and "the last."[1]

The Suffering Servant may also be placed within this forward movement of the LORD's purposes on a broad historical canvas. Within chapters 40–55 a certain progression can be discerned. The servant is identified as Israel in Isaiah 41:8 for the first time in the book and in the Old Testament. This locates him within the tradition of Israel as the LORD's chosen people. But in the course of chapters 41–53 his mission takes a distinctive shape: his destiny is to "bring forth justice to the nations" (42:1). While bringing light to the nations, he is also called (strangely) "to raise up the tribes of Jacob, and restore those who have been preserved in Israel" (49:6). He is then depicted as suffering at the hands of others in the course of discharging his duties as a teacher (50:4–9). Finally, this suffering is seen to have a purpose in bearing the sins of others and in leading to a renewal of life, even beyond the grave (52:13–53:12). The servant, therefore, emerges out of the story of Israel, yet within the story he becomes something entirely new.

This new thing is enormously significant for the book of Isaiah. It means that its trajectory is no simple progression from disaster to triumph. Rather, the destiny of servant-Israel is to be realized only through suffering. Yet the book declines to disclose the nature of this suffering apart from the terms of the poem itself. This means that the story of the servant cannot be understood as an incident, some one-off event on the timeline leading to the glorification of Zion. Instead, it is embedded in

---

1. For the former and latter things, see Isa. 41:22; 42:9; 43:18; cf. 52:4. For the LORD himself, see 44:6; 48:12.

the Isaianic conception of how God works in history. That has at its heart the LORD's sovereignty over historical events. Empires rise and fall in succession at his behest. But the Suffering Servant adds a distinctive dimension to this picture. The God who ordains the rise and fall of empires has placed his servant into the flow of events as a key to their deepest meaning. A human being having an intimate connection with the LORD himself suffers the deadly assaults of hatred and violence, only to emerge through them victorious and open up fresh vistas of life and the good to "many." In the conception of the book of Isaiah, this is a depiction of the deepest reality, the way things really are in God's world.

It hardly needs saying that this vision of the way things truly are in God's world runs completely counter to notions of power and reality that prevailed in biblical times and still do in ours. The book of Isaiah, from start to finish, exposes the delusions of power. In Isaiah's day, Assyrians and Babylonians made claims about themselves that mimicked the claims of God. They believed in their own invincibility, as did the lesser nations around them that looked out at their huge armies in glittering array and thought that in them lay the world's real power. In the message of Isaiah, such pretensions are shown repeatedly to be vacuous. The narrative of Isaiah 36–37 deconstructs such self-obsessed folly with brilliant irony. Yet the delusion seems doomed to endless repetition. We still live in a world in which unimaginably massive armaments are designed to say, *We* have the power of life and death; we alone can bring destruction or security on our terms and at our whim. This picture is replicated from the superpower level down through the world's petty, repressive fiefdoms.

Yet there is an insecurity at the heart of this world-picture. It comes from an inkling of a deeper reality and a wary eye on the gospel of Christ and its subversive power to throw all the cards in the air. Those with an interest in the status quo knew this in the time of the first Christians, when religious leaders complained to a Roman official in Thessalonica that Paul and Silas had "turned the world upside down," and saw with clarity that Jesus threatened the foundations of Caesar's rule (Acts 17:6–8). Isaiah uses a similar metaphor in Isaiah 29:16. This is why oppressive powers have always sought means to neutralize the gospel, whether by absorbing it into narratives of national destiny or by ruthless repression. Stories of the martyrs, from Stephen in Acts 7 to more recent truth-tellers like Dietrich Bonhoeffer in Hitler's Germany, Jerzy Popiełuszko in Communist Poland, and Archbishop Janani Luwum in Idi Amin's Uganda, testify eloquently to jumpy dictators' fear of the gospel. But the dangers come in less dramatic ways too, not least today by taming the message of Christ into sly self-improvement mythologies.

A Question of Truth

At the heart of the book of Isaiah and the message of the servant, as we have already observed, is the question of truth. Or perhaps "Truth" should be spelled with a capital T in the light of Jesus's saying, "I am the way, the T/truth, and the life" (John 14:6). It is truth that is everywhere at stake, and everywhere contested, in the book of Isaiah. This is evident in its very style, predominantly the rhetorical style with poetic forms common to the Old Testament prophets. The premise throughout is that the people who hear the prophetic words, or who read them long after they were spoken, are mired in misconceptions and that these misconceptions need to be addressed in ways that powerfully challenge the heart and mind to see things differently. The scene is set in Isaiah 1:2–3, in which the people of Israel are described, with heavy irony, as children who have rebelled, whose knowledge and understanding of their real situation may be compared unfavorably with that of an ox or a donkey. The key text for the motif of seeing, hearing, and understanding is Isaiah 6:9–10:

> And he said: "Go and say to this people: 'Keep on hearing, but you will not understand! Keep on seeing, but you will not attain knowledge.' Make the minds of this people thick, their ears dull and their eyes blind, lest they see with their eyes, hear with their ears, and understand with their minds, lest they repent and are healed!"

This arresting language is often mistaken for a kind of divine determinism, with the prophet's speech as its instrument. On the contrary, however, everything recorded in the prophetic witness aims at response and new understanding. The pervasive hope of the prophetic speech is to bring about a meeting of minds between wayward people and the LORD himself. As the LORD says, again in the first chapter, "Come, let us think rightly about this" (Isa. 1:18). The line is better known as "Come now, and let us reason together," as in KJV, with echoes in several more recent translations. The sense of the line is hard to convey, but "reasoning together" smacks too much, in my view, of a polite, roundtable discussion, given that the speech continues as a call to obedience, with life itself at stake. Yet the "let us" form of address is crucially important, for it speaks of the LORD's self-identification with people. He is committed to their life and good, their sins forgiven and put behind (1:18–20). And he shows this by engaging with them through speech that is designed to reach and convert their hearts and minds. There is an incarnational aspect of this, which comes to fuller expression in due course with the servant.

The unfolding "story" of Isaiah illustrates the extent of human resistance to the LORD's truth. Some of its most memorable passages express the discrepancy between the LORD's vision and the people's contrary direction. In the parable of the vineyard, the LORD looks for righteousness (*ṣədāqâ*) but, in an ironic parody, finds only "a cry" (*ṣəʿāqâ*), the cry of the oppressed betokening a perversion of the truth that should have taken practical shape in a just society. Active resistance to the truth is also the dominant theme in Isaiah 28, in which the people's leaders in Jerusalem are depicted as drunk and confused, unable to see straight or make right decisions (28:7–8). Against this backdrop, the LORD's "teaching of knowledge" (v. 9) is a perplexing conundrum. For the rulers, it has become a derisory repetition of meaningless sounds (v. 13). So far are they from knowledge of the truth that they are depicted as willfully committed to lies: "When the overwhelming scourge passes over, it will not come upon us, for we have made deceit our refuge, and taken cover behind a lie" (v. 15). They have, by their own admission, made a "covenant with death" (vv. 15, 18), where "death" is an animated, godlike force;[2] their "covenant" is therefore the very antithesis of the covenants that God had made with Israel through Abraham (Gen. 15), Moses (Exod. 19–24), and David (2 Sam. 7; 23:5–7).

The problem pervasively confronted in Isaiah is that of "seeming truth." People who are deeply deluded think they are perceiving the real facts about the way things are in the world. This is what was exploited in the rhetoric in the passage noted above (Isa. 36–37). It is an extraordinarily pertinent analysis of the modern world as well, with its "alternative facts," "fake news," and the cynical fantasies of demagogues who can hold

---

2. Again, in ancient Canaan the word "death" (*môt*) was also the name of the god Mot, who symbolized the most profound danger to all life. The cognate Hebrew term *māwet* has the same potential range of meaning.

whole populations in thrall. As I write this, in the year of our Lord 2022, we are seeing daily the endlessly violent and destructive manifestations of "seeming truth."

This is why Cyrus cannot ultimately save us; only the servant can do so. In Isaiah 53, the truth (Truth) is embodied in the figure who takes upon and into himself the lies and violence of the world. That he should do so, and in doing so bear the burden of the sins of "the many," is so outrageous that it has all the appearance of a fantastic untruth. Yet it transpires that this alone is true, and the untruth actually lies in the easy plausibilities that pose as ways of wisdom.

There is in the narrative arc of Isaiah a motif of waiting. The prophet himself, sealing up some of his words and entrusting them to his "learners" (*limmuday*, "my learners/disciples") for a future disclosure of their truth, declares that he will "wait for the LORD," who is at that time "hiding his face" from Israel (Isa. 8:16–17). When the servant in due course makes his appearance in the book, it is a response to this long waiting. That waiting has been partly fulfilled by the punishment and subsequent restoration of Israel to its land, the theme initiated in chapter 40. But the arc of expectation is picked up expressly by the servant too, when he describes himself as a "learner" (*limmûd*, 50:4), in an echo of Isaiah's "learners" in 8:16. This "learner" is also a teacher. But only in Isaiah 53 comes the real denouement of this narrative of discipleship. The "teaching" is embodied in a servant who goes silently and submissively to an unjust death. This atrocity, starkly contrary to all sense or reasonable expectation, is *the* Truth.

I have described a "narrative" in the book of Isaiah. It is not a narrative in the strict sense, of course. Nor is there, formally, a single denouement. The image of the Suffering Servant is not an "end" in the sense of "happily ever after," but rather a moment of revelation that changes everything permanently, giving shape irreversibly to all life and thought.

The sense of an ending[3] in the book of Isaiah is not given in a single place. It is carried, for example, in the motifs we have noticed above: of "newness," or "new things," running through chapters 40–55 and culminating in "new heavens and a new earth" (65:17; 66:22);[4] and in the vision of a great banquet on Mount Zion (25:6), the lifting of an obscuring veil from all people, and the swallowing up of death forever (vv. 7–8)—all this as God's salvation for which "we" have waited (v. 9). These are endings that still look forward and that feed into a waiting that continues. They are not in competition with each other. Rather, our concepts of the heavenly banquet and of new heavens and a new earth are unavoidably imbued with the image of the Suffering Servant.

Preaching and Reading the Servant Today

It will be clear what a challenge it is to preach and teach Isaiah 53. It is inextricable from the dominant thrust of the whole biblical story, with its radical hostility to worldly conceptions of status, privilege, and power. Consequently, it is difficult to reflect on it apart from its place in that story, as has been evident in the remarks made so far in the present chapter.

Yet the poem makes a unique contribution to the story. In teaching and preaching it, how may we do justice to the individuality of its conception, while at the same time acknowledging its indissoluble connection, in Christian thinking, to Jesus Christ? In faithfulness to biblical interpretation, we should not

---

3. The phrase is borrowed from the novel *The Sense of an Ending* by Julian Barnes (2011), with its hint that the idea of an "ending" is problematical.
4. See also Isa. 42:9–10; 43:19; 48:6.

miss the lineaments of the poem itself. It may be that an honest attempt to expound this wonderful scripture is bound to be somewhat bifocal. Christian preachers on Isaiah 53 may face a dilemma. In what way can they be true to the poem while at the same time paying attention to the servant's distinctive realization in Christ?

We have seen that there is not a unitary reception of the poem. Its New Testament readers used it in the contexts of their own instruction and exhortation, resulting in the variety we find in the New Testament. If they could zoom in on angles in the poem, perhaps we are free to do the same. Or it may be better to think of a process by which we move back and forth between the poem itself and its New Testament receptions.

I want now to suggest three ways in which we might develop this idea homiletically.

1. Contemplation

It is not incidental to Isaiah 53 that it is a poem. I hope to have brought out some of its poetic force as an act of communication. As a work of imagination, it lays hold of us, not just intellectually, but in its emotive appeal. These levels do not exist in separate compartments, of course, as I argued above (in chap. 2). The power of poetry lies in its understanding of human complexity: we grasp a thing with heart, mind, and soul.

The poem makes its strongest impact, I think, in its portrayal of human suffering. When the picture is unfolded in 53:1–9, questions of identity, time, place, and circumstance retreat behind the sheer presence of a suffering human being. This skillful poetic effect is akin to what the ancient Greek rhetoricians called *pathos*, the engagement of the audience's emotional participation and assent. (The term occurs in English in a word such as "sympathy.") The poet uses artful devices to achieve his aim: rhetorical questions (v. 1), metaphors (vv. 2, 6, 7), an appeal to the (admittedly culturally specific) values of disgust and beauty (v. 2), a narrative of severe physical and psychological abuse (vv. 3–5), and the identification of speaker with audience in the use of "we" and "us," which gathers momentum in verses 4–6 and compels the hearers or readers to see that this terrible image presented to their view did not belong in a remote place, but had everything to do with themselves.

The poem focuses brilliantly on the humanity of the servant. We considered something of this notion in the preceding chapter, noting not only its theological significance for the humanity of Christ but also the compelling power of its depiction, for example, in the type of visual art labeled loosely as "man of sorrows." For the preacher, this opens up opportunities. There is a place for focusing on the suffering of Christ, in proper, humble awe before his pain and in keeping with a long history of artistic depiction of the cross. (There is also a danger of being excessively lurid, which the sensitive preacher and teacher will know how to avoid. The poem maintains a fine balance between looking and looking away.)

But there are other kinds of opportunities too. We are confronted daily with images of human suffering: from war, hunger, cruelty, the loss of a child, a devastating diagnosis, a ruined hope, abandonment by lover or friend. In ordinary daily experience, the world's pain did not end at Calvary. Jesus was not the last to cry, "My God, why have you forsaken me?" The portrait of the servant, because it is so carefully loosened from time and place, has a universal quality that gives it affinities with all of these. It is an invitation to alertness to a world still marked deeply by tragedy. And this quality has an appeal to readers of every stamp, simply by virtue of their humanity. That is, the poem's impact is not essentially dependent on seeing it through specifically Christian lenses. This is an aspect of its interpretation in which Christians and Jews in particular may share common ground.[5]

Attention to the suffering of the world may lead to all kinds of responses, from grief to prayer to various kinds of action. The poem itself gives a specific prompt, prior to all of these, to self-knowledge. The confession of the "we" speakers says much about the human capacity for self-deception. People can live untroubled in bubbles of health and prosperity, sometimes for years. But the speakers' example compels us to look critically at the ways in which we deceive ourselves and at how we relate to the unfairness and cruelties of the world.

2. Death and New Life

The poem does not rest with the portrait of the servant's suffering, or even his death, but dramatically turns a corner. The servant will live, be satisfied, see offspring, and turn people to the right way. Having borne their sins, he leads them into a new kind of future. For just this reason, the book of Isaiah has been called the "fifth gospel."

How may we deal with this transition in the poem? In one vital sense, we are bound to do so in relation to the resurrection of Christ after his passion and death, which is the basis of all Christian hope. Yet, as readers of Isaiah 53, we must still come to terms with this stark contrast between the harrowing portrait and the promised renewal of life. How can we handle both the

---

5. Brettler and Levine document some postbiblical Jewish readings of Isa. 53. It is noteworthy that Jewish readings do not necessarily adopt a corporate interpretation of the servant. Indeed, "early rabbinic texts generally understood the servant as an individual rather than as collective Israel" ("Isaiah's Suffering Servant," 169). However, they also note that at least one talmudic text "understand[s] the servant to be anyone whom God deems to so punish," citing b. Ber. 5a (170). I find this interesting because of the universality implied in "anyone," rather than the note about punishment.

tragedy and the joy? Is it acceptable, as a matter of conscience, to celebrate the good things of life against the horizon of suffering in the world? How does one go from a funeral to a wedding?

In fact, the poem does not allow us to pull these things apart. As readers, we are strongly led to make that sharp transition from death to life in 53:9–10. This too is part of the reality that it conveys. The poem's vision is unified, with the focus in verses 10–12 remaining on the servant. Characteristically, however, it continues to be somewhat enigmatic: In what way will he "see his offspring"? What does it mean that he will be "satisfied by his knowledge"? How is he to "make many righteous," and how does that relate to his "bearing their sins"? The tone of verses 10–12 is curiously nontriumphalistic, notwithstanding the metaphor of taking booty after battle in verse 12a. It is not expressly joyful. The emphasis falls instead on fathoming the meaning of the servant's life. The mystery of it is maintained in the idea that it was the LORD's will that he should suffer, yet that he himself "poured out his life." The fine balance between the servant's act of self-sacrifice and the benefits brought to others is maintained to the end. And the poem finishes with a new idea, what seems to be his ongoing activity of making intercession for sinners or "rebels" (v. 12c).

The depiction of the servant's survival and his new and productive life never loses sight of his suffering. His self-sacrifice and death for the sake of others are still in view in the final verse. Our reception of the poem has somehow to embrace this unity of death and life. We noticed in some post–Old Testament reception of Isaiah 53 a certain hesitation between the vicarious suffering and the triumphant messiah, as if one of these must yield to the other. Yet the poem scarcely permits such polarization.

How do we go from a funeral to a wedding? It is a troubling question. Yet it illustrates the important point that both sorrow and joy are woven together in human experience. The possibility of joy and celebration is grounded, for the Christian, in the resurrection and the hope that it brings. It is also inseparable from the cross of Christ. The link between cross and resurrection is unbreakable. Joy and hope are possible because the worst has been faced and dealt with. The unity of this conception is signaled right at the start of the poem, when the LORD declares that the servant "will be high and lifted up, and greatly exalted" (52:13), terms that are otherwise reserved for the LORD alone. This glorification of the servant is set as the goal, before we even come to the depiction of his anguish. The ending of the poem thus corresponds to its beginning, with a forward look toward the benefits that the servant's sacrificial love has achieved. To the contemplation of suffering humanity that dominated 53:1–9 may be counterpoised the contemplation of glory. John's Gospel expresses this paradox in a distinctive way, as we saw in the preceding chapter, with its convergence of Christ's lifting up on the cross and his lifting up to glory (e.g., John 12:28–32). Christian liturgy expresses it in the memorial repetition from Good Friday to Easter of the last days of Jesus, from his crucifixion to his resurrection. Yet Easter services, in my experience, often include a Eucharist, in which the crucifixion still plays a central part.

These approaches to the unifying of suffering and glory are not neat solutions to a thorny problem. There are questions that are not easily answered. Why was it necessary for the servant to suffer in order to "bear our sins"? The poem does not answer this. And it sits oddly with Isaiah 40:1–2, which proclaims the restoration of Israel after the punishment of exile, with the assurance to Jerusalem

> that she has served her term,
> that her penalty is paid,

> that she has received from the LORD's hand
> double for all her sins. (NRSV)

What Isaiah 53 does do is to suggest that the servant's suffering achieved things that would otherwise not have been achieved. The problem that the book of Isaiah repeatedly identifies could not be solved merely by overcoming the historical enemies of Israel and restoring the exiles to Jerusalem. The prophet has exposed an unyielding resistance to the ways of God, even among his people, which continues in some measure to the end of the book. As already noted, Cyrus could not solve this chronic problem. This is not to eliminate Cyrus from the picture. The dialectic of tension between "Cyrus" and "servant" does not end with the book of Isaiah or even with the New Testament. The life of the servant in the history of the church has taken shape variously in relation to a host of earthly powers. But in the silencing of kings and the suggestion that they will come to new vision and understanding (52:15) lies something more profound than the punitive overthrow of the arrogant that is a common theme in Isaiah. The idea that the LORD's servant, the "righteous one," has suffered as far as death in order to "make many righteous" exceeds all mere prophetic exhortations to be righteous. Isaiah 53 uniquely places into the story of sin and salvation an innocent human figure who, by his willing suffering and self-sacrifice, bears the sins of others. This is the perpetual witness of the church to the world.

But must it be so? Must there be pain for the world to be the best it can be? Theologians have grappled with the question of whether the whole tragic human story was a necessary precondition of ultimate salvation. Our only answer to such questions comes in the form of the narrative and contemplation of the cross and resurrection. This is our way into an understanding of how things really are in God's world. The essence and the end of that reality is in glorification after the harshness of life. It is perhaps poets and spiritual writers who come closest to catching the mystery of this. Jessica Martin writes, "Paradise is a place of mercy and restoration, where tears are wiped away, rather than that they were never shed."[6] And Malcolm Guite, in the closing lines of his poem on Christ's transfiguration (Mark 9:2–8), sees it as a foretaste of his resurrection glory:

> Nor can this blackened sky, this darkened scar,
> Eclipse that glimpse of how things really are.[7]

There is no going back behind the suffering of Christ or the suffering of the world. There is only the glimpse of glory that is at the end. In Isaiah's language, those who are open to the vision "shall see . . . and understand" (Isa. 52:15).

3. Servant / Servants

I said above that everything written in Isaiah is intended to produce a response in reader and hearer. In Isaiah 53 this does not take the form of an open call to repent and change. The poet allows the poem itself, in its structure, theme, and language, to do the work of persuasion. The portrait of the servant does have an inescapably didactic aspect, since it leads into the topics of substitution/representation in atonement and of surviving death. It was, of course, its theme and substance that made the poem so pertinent to the first Christians' articulation of the meaning of Christ. Yet the poem does not function as a handbook to settle theological controversies around the nature or reach of Christ's atoning death for others. It calls

---

6. Martin, *Holiness and Desire*, 33. She cites Ps. 30:5 [6] in support.
7. Guite, "Transfiguration," in *Sounding the Seasons*, 56.

instead for sympathetic engagement and active response. I have indicated some possible responses above. But there is also an exemplary aspect to the portrait of the servant. This is evident in the poem's setting in the latter part of Isaiah, in which a connection is made between the servant and "servants," first in the immediately following chapter (54:17), then in 63:17 and 65:13–16. These latter texts apparently testify to a distinction made within the restored postexilic community between those in Israel who are faithful and deserve the name of "servant," and those who are not. If these texts testify to some historical conflict, it cannot be confidently described. But the crucial point is that the servant in Isaiah 53 has become a model with which others wanted to identify. The story of the servant not only raises questions of who and how; it also sets an example.

The example is enormously solemn. The words "servant" and "service" are common and frequent in contemporary use, and in some cases have settled into conventional phrases such as "civil servant," or "your obedient servant," or even "the armed services." "Service" can have stronger connotations, as when a person is honored for a lifetime of dedicated service to a worthy cause or effort. I write these words in the week in which Queen Elizabeth II, the United Kingdom's longest-reigning monarch, has died. Her youthful promise of lifelong service to her nation has been frequently cited in the days following her death. The concept takes on a certain resonance when it is combined with royal power. Seen as the dedication of a life, its nature is less a series of helpful acts than something existential. In the deepest sense, service is self-sacrificial.

In biblical times, kings could be styled "servants of God." As we already observed (chap. 1), in one place the LORD calls King Nebuchadnezzar of Babylon "my servant" (Jer. 27:6). The term is applied to King David in Isaiah 37:35. The royal-messianic figure in Isaiah 11:1–5 has important affinities with the servant of the LORD, as we have seen in Isaiah 40–55. This figure has the spirit of the LORD in him, with wisdom and understanding and a commission to bring justice to the earth (cf. Isa. 42:1–4; 53:11). The servant of the LORD, though never described as a king, carries connotations of kingship with him because of these resonances. Yet there is no claim to grandeur here. Service as self-sacrifice reaches its most sublime expression in this individual, destined to be "highly exalted" like the LORD himself (52:13), but one who exerts no forceful power and offers himself as a sacrifice. How radical a thought this is can hardly be overstated. It is an inversion of normal conceptions and expectations of power. Greatness in a ruler is often associated with historic victories, expansion of territory, even war. The servant in Isaiah belies such things. His path to glory is through renunciation. The idea is so counterintuitive that it can only be grasped by faith, faith that is prepared to risk the loss of life itself. It is a point that is well to have in mind when, perhaps in song, we call upon the LORD to "show his power."

The New Testament writers found in Christ this model of service as sacrifice, as exemplified by Paul's wonderful hymn on Christ's self-emptying and glorification (Phil. 2:6–11). Strikingly, he sets it in the context of an exhortation to his addressees to be "like-minded" (v. 2) or, in other words, to practice humility toward each other. They too are to "take the form of a servant." In Mark's Gospel, Jesus takes up the theme when he declares that "the Son of Man came not to be served but to serve" (Mark 10:45), in a passage that continues with a close echo of Isaiah 53:10–12: "and to give his life as a ransom for many." And similarly, Jesus calls his disciples to "take up their cross" and follow him (Mark 8:34). One of the striking things about the portrayal of the servant's experience is that it involves learning. He comes to see the fruit of his tribulations, and it is by his "knowledge" that he makes many righteous (Isa. 53:11). The servant knows more about his servanthood at the end than at the beginning.

▓ Final Reflections

I argued above that Isaiah 53 is unlike the Old Testament's rich literature of lamentation in the sense that the human suffering depicted is not made a cause of protest or appeal to God. It certainly takes its place among the great lamentations of Job, Psalms, and the book of Lamentations itself as a depiction of perplexing anguish. Yet there is something here that goes beyond lament. The silent servant does not protest. Rather, the presiding mood borders on wonder. It is astonishing that a powerless and humiliated human being should be designated by God as his servant and destined to be highly exalted. The wonder of it is further expressed by the group that speaks as "we" in 53:1–6, who have come to realize what had initially seemed to them incredible: that this one whom they had deemed an outcast, justly condemned by God, was in fact suffering in their stead and was an instrument of God for the restitution of things whose scope they could barely comprehend. There is wonder too at the servant's willing, silent acceptance of his affliction, to which God set no limit, not even death. All this was somehow "the will of the LORD" (53:10).

This is not to say that the servant's anguish is somehow only instrumental, to be passed over lightly on the way to the good news at the end. On the contrary, the "man of sorrows" motif has been rightly taken up as an icon of the perennial subjection of the human to the most callous horrors imaginable. But what is special about Isaiah 53 is that the presence of God is somehow woven into the story, and that the whole tragedy is conceived as a pathway to the unlimited good of "many." This thought carries dangers with it. It should not be taken to mean that God has created evil in order that good might come. Christian theology has always avoided this step, and we must not draw inferences from Isaiah 53 that the text does not warrant. Equally to be avoided is the idea that God was subject to some kind of necessity in order to bring about his ultimate good purposes, as if God could be constrained by anything outside himself. More modestly, the text may hint that the experience of suffering and evil can lead to deeper and richer outcomes than there might otherwise have been. But even that thought needs caution, since many situations are simply unbearable and unrelieved. Often we can say only that God is always in and with the suffering, and simultaneously declare that suffering is not the final word.

There is inevitably, therefore, an eschatological dimension to our reading of the servant-poem. Wedged into the ongoing and unfinished story unfolded by the book of Isaiah, the poem points beyond itself. Its truth concerns the deepest relations between God, humanity, and the world and is therefore a token of all that the Bible conveys to us of God's ways. This is the message of the cross and resurrection of Christ.

We might also discern a trinitarian aspect to the poem. By this I do not mean that it discloses a fully formed doctrine of the Trinity. That does not occur anywhere in the Old Testament. However, a certain trinitarian shape can be discerned in the poem's concept. The action is initiated by the LORD; the focus falls on a human figure whose life, death, and new life achieve the LORD's purpose to save; and the meaning of the events portrayed is in a true perception given (in an unspoken way) to the speakers in verses 1–6 and to the poet himself. In trinitarian terms, this is the work of the Spirit. There is also the closest affinity between the LORD and his servant, so that in their own ways they have willed the servant's self-sacrificial suffering and its character as a substitution (or "exchange"), by which he bears the sins of others.

The point has been made above and needs only to be glossed by a hermeneutical rider. Christian readings of Isaiah 53 do not consist only in unpacking the poem's christological significance. It is not simply a signpost saying, "This points to that." I hope that what we have seen of the poem's artful composition and evocative power has conveyed something of its capacity to produce all kinds of responses. At one level, it tells us of things that have happened and that will happen. But it does not merely inform. The story of the servant calls readers to servant-like response. What this might be in any case is a matter of judgment, perception, and imagination rather than mere obedience to command. But in grasping it, we will be in touch with the deepest understanding of what it means to be human in God's world.

Bibliography

Ådna, Jostein. "The Servant of Isaiah 53 as Triumphant and Interceding Messiah: The Reception of Isaiah 52:13–53:12 in the Targum of Isaiah with Special Attention to the Concept of the Messiah." In Janowski and Stuhlmacher, *Suffering Servant*, 189–224.

Alter, Robert. *The Art of Biblical Narrative*. New York: Basic Books, 1981.

———. *The Art of Biblical Poetry*. New York: Basic Books, 1985.

Bellinger, William H., and William R. Farmer, eds. *Jesus and the Suffering Servant: Isaiah 53 and Christian Origins*. Harrisburg, PA: Trinity Press International, 1998.

Betz, Otto. "Jesus and Isaiah 53." In Bellinger and Farmer, *Jesus and the Suffering Servant*, 70–87.

Brettler, Marc, and Amy-Jill Levine. "Isaiah's Suffering Servant: Before and After Christianity." *Interpretation* 73, no. 2 (2019): 158–73.

Briggs, Richard S. *The Lord Is My Shepherd: Psalm 23 for the Life of the Church*. Grand Rapids: Baker Academic, 2021.

Brueggemann, Walter. *Cadences of Home: Preaching among Exiles*. Louisville: Westminster John Knox, 1998.

———. *The Prophetic Imagination*. 40th anniv. ed. Minneapolis: Fortress, 2018.

Carroll R., M. Daniel. *The Lord Roars: Recovering the Prophetic Voice for Today*. Grand Rapids: Baker Academic, 2022.

Chapman, Stephen. "Reclaiming Inspiration for the Bible." In *Canon and Biblical Interpretation*, edited by Craig Bartholomew et al., 167–206.

Scripture and Hermeneutics Series 7. Milton Keynes: Paternoster; Grand Rapids: Zondervan, 2006.

Childs, Brevard. *Biblical Theology of the Old and New Testaments*. Minneapolis: Fortress, 1993.

Clines, David J. A. *I, He, We, and They: A Literary Approach to Isaiah 53*. Journal for the Study of the Old Testament Supplement Series 1. Sheffield: JSOT Press, 1976.

Coleridge, Samuel Taylor. *Biographia Literaria*. Vol. 7 of The Collected Works of Samuel Taylor Coleridge. Edited by James Engell and W. Jackson Bate. Princeton: Princeton University Press, 1983.

Cornwell, John, ed. *Nature's Imagination: The Frontiers of Scientific Vision*. Oxford: Oxford University Press, 1995.

Cranfield, C. E. B. *The Epistle to the Romans*. Vol. 1, *I–VIII*. International Critical Commentary. Edinburgh: T&T Clark, 1975.

Delitzsch, Franz. *The Prophecies of Isaiah*, vol. 2. Translated by James Martin. Grand Rapids: Eerdmans, 1973.

de Vaux, Roland. *Ancient Israel: Its Life and Institutions*. New York: McGraw-Hill, 1961.

Ford, David F. *Christian Wisdom: Desiring God and Learning in Love*. Cambridge: Cambridge University Press, 2007.

Frei, Hans W. *The Eclipse of Biblical Narrative: A Study in Eighteenth and Nineteenth Century Hermeneutics*. New Haven: Yale University Press, 1974.

Geyser-Fouché, A. B., and T. M. Munengwa. "The Concept of Vicarious Suffering in the Old Testament." *HTS Teologiese Studies/Theological Studies* 75, no. 4 (2019), a5352. https://doi.org/10.4102/hts.v75i4.5352.

Goldingay, John. *The Message of Isaiah 40–55: A Literary-Theological Commentary*. London: T&T Clark, 2005.

Green, Garrett. *Imagining Theology: Encounters with God in Scripture, Interpretation, and Aesthetics*. Grand Rapids: Baker Academic, 2020.

Guite, Malcolm. *Lifting the Veil: Imagination and the Kingdom of God*. Norwich: Canterbury Press, 2022.

———. *Sounding the Seasons: Seventy Sonnets for the Christian Year*. London: Canterbury Press, 2012.

Gunton, Colin E. *The Actuality of Atonement: A Study of Metaphor, Rationality, and the Christian Tradition*. London and New York: T&T Clark, 1998.

Hengel, Martin, with Daniel P. Bailey. "The Effective History of Isaiah 53 in the Pre-Christian Period." In Janowski and Stuhlmacher, *Suffering Servant*, 75–146.

Hooker, Morna D. "Did the Use of Isaiah 53 to Interpret His Mission Begin with Jesus?" In Bellinger and Farmer, *Jesus and the Suffering Servant*, 88–103.

Horbury, William. "The Wisdom of Solomon." In *The Oxford Bible Commentary*, edited by John Barton and John Muddiman, 650–67. Oxford: Oxford University Press, 2001.

Janowski, Bernd. "He Bore Our Sins: Isaiah 53 and the Drama of Taking Another's Place." In Janowski and Stuhlmacher, *Suffering Servant*, 48–74.

Janowski, Bernd, and Peter Stuhlmacher. *The Suffering Servant: Isaiah 53 in Jewish and Christian Sources*. Grand Rapids: Eerdmans, 2004.

Jenson, P. P. *Graded Holiness: A Key to the Priestly Conception of the World*. Journal for the Study of the Old Testament Supplement Series 106. Sheffield: JSOT Press, 1992.

Koole, Jan L. *Isaiah III*. Vol. 2, *Isaiah 49–55*. Historical Commentary on the Old Testament. Leuven: Peeters, 1998.

Lambert, W. G. *Babylonian Wisdom Literature*. Oxford: Clarendon, 1960.

Levenson, Jon D. *Resurrection and the Restoration of Israel: The Ultimate Victory of the God of Life*. New Haven: Yale University Press, 2006.

Levison, Jack. *Inspired: The Holy Spirit and the Mind of Faith*. Grand Rapids: Eerdmans, 2013.

Lincoln, Andrew T. *The Gospel according to Saint John*. Black's New Testament Commentary. Grand Rapids: Baker Academic, 2005.

Martin, Jessica. *Holiness and Desire*. Norwich: Canterbury Press, 2020.

McConville, J. Gordon. *Isaiah*. BCOT. Grand Rapids: Baker Academic, 2023.

Midgley, Mary. *The Myths We Live By*. London and New York: Routledge, 2004.

———. *Science and Poetry*. London and New York: Routledge, 2001.

Nolland, John. *Luke 18:35–24:53*. Word Biblical Commentary. Dallas: Word, 1993.

Paul, Shalom M. *Isaiah 40–66*. Eerdmans Critical Commentary. Grand Rapids: Eerdmans, 2012.

Powery, Emerson B. *The Good Samaritan: Luke 10 for the Life of the Church*. Grand Rapids: Baker Academic, 2022.

Ricoeur, Paul. "The Nuptial Metaphor." In *Thinking Biblically: Exegetical and Hermeneutical Studies*, edited by André Lacocque and Paul Ricoeur, 267–300. Chicago: University of Chicago Press, 1998.

———. *The Rule of Metaphor: Multidisciplinary Studies of the Creation of Meaning in Language.* Toronto: University of Toronto Press, 1977.

Rutledge, Fleming. *The Crucifixion: Understanding the Death of Jesus Christ.* Grand Rapids: Eerdmans, 2015.

Saenger, Paul. "The Anglo-Hebraic Origins of the Modern Chapter Division of the Latin Bible." In *La fractura historiografica: Edad Media y Renacimento desde el tercer milenio*, edited by Francesco Javier Burguillo and Laura Meier, 177–202. Salamanca: Seminario de Estudios Medievales y Renacentistas, 2008.

Sawyer, John F. A. *The Fifth Gospel: Isaiah in the History of Christianity.* Cambridge: Cambridge University Press, 1996.

Schiller, G. *Iconography of Christian Art.* London: Lund Humphries, 1972.

Schipper, Jeremy. "Interpreting the Lamb Imagery in Isaiah 53." *Journal of Biblical Literature* 132 (2013): 315–25.

Seitz, Christopher. *The Elder Testament: Canon, Theology, Trinity.* Waco: Baylor University Press, 2018.

Sonderegger, Katherine. *Systematic Theology.* Vol. 1, *The Doctrine of God.* Minneapolis: Fortress, 2015.

Strawn, Brent A. *The Old Testament Is Dying: A Diagnosis and Recommended Treatment.* Grand Rapids: Baker Academic, 2017.

Thiselton, Anthony C. *The First Epistle to the Corinthians.* New International Greek Testament Commentary. Grand Rapids: Eerdmans, 2000.

VanderKam, James C. *The Dead Sea Scrolls and the Bible.* Grand Rapids: Eerdmans, 2012.

Volf, Miroslav. *Exclusion and Embrace: A Theological Exploration of Identity, Otherness, and Reconciliation.* Nashville: Abingdon, 1996.

Westermann, Claus. *Isaiah 40–66: A Commentary.* Translated by D. M. G. Stalker. Old Testament Library. Philadelphia: Westminster, 1969.

Whybray, R. N. *Thanksgiving for a Liberated Prophet: An Interpretation of Isaiah Chapter 53.* Journal for the Study of the Old Testament Supplement Series 4. Sheffield: JSOT Press, 1978.

Wilde, Oscar. *"De Profundis," "The Ballad of Reading Gaol," and Other Writings.* Edited by Anne Varty. Wordsworth Classics. Ware, Hertfordshire: Wordsworth Editions, 2002.

Williams, Catrin. "Another Look at 'Lifting Up' in the Gospel of John." In *Conception, Reception, and the Spirit: Essays in Honor of Andrew T. Lincoln*, edited by J. Gordon McConville and Lloyd K. Pietersen, 58–70. Eugene, OR: Cascade Books, 2015.

Witherington, Ben, III. *Isaiah Old and New: Exegesis, Intertextuality, and Hermeneutics*. Minneapolis: Fortress, 2017.

Wright, Christopher J. H. *God's People in God's Land: Family, Land, and Property in the Old Testament*. Grand Rapids: Eerdmans, 1990.

Wright, N. T. *Paul and the Faithfulness of God*. Christian Origins and the Question of God 4. London: SPCK, 2013.

Scripture Index

Subject Index